Exploring I

A study guide from the Masters of the Spirit World

Exploring Reincarnation

Library of Congress Control Number: 2011909746

ISBN: 978-0-9829529-5-5

Published by Celestial Voices, Inc.,
13354 W. Heiden Circle, Lake Bluff, Illinois 60044

FIRST EDITION
(Paperback)

Metaphysics - the philosophy of being

Exploring

Reincarnation

A study guide from the Masters of the Spirit World

Peter Watson Jenkins, MA, MH

Toni Ann Winninger, JD, CH

~ Celestial Voices, Inc. ~

The purpose of this book

The Masters of the Spirit World present this metaphysical study of reincarnation as their principal teaching manual on the topic. The book contains information that human beings may desire to know about the purpose of the soul as it shuttles, life after life, age after age, between this planet and its spiritual Home in the fifth dimension.

Our world listens to many diverse voices telling us what the universe is like, speculating on the nature of divinity and on the purpose of the soul. In the midst of much uncertainty and guesswork, the Masters' teaching resonates with the natural authority of those who teach what they know is true.

The Masters, the real authors of this book, have recruited spokespeople Toni Ann Winninger to channel their words, and Peter Watson Jenkins to edit and present their teaching. Sonia Ness and Robert Buzek have added their own valuable contributions to ensure the text is accurate and the cover beautiful. The manuscript was reviewed by the Masters and has been given their final approval.

It is what you *feel* about this book that counts most in your reading of it, the Masters say. With no compulsion to believe, and no religious organization to join, the book is, simply, enlightened teaching, made available for this stage of your journey. The Masters hope you will enjoy it.

Contents:

Acknowledgments

Sonia A. Ness
for her copy editing

Robert Buzek
for his cover design

Introduction

What is reincarnation? There's a lot of nonsense talked about this major metaphysical mystery, and it's time to put the record straight. First, to be clear, the word itself means "back in the flesh" (flesh implying a physical human body).

Many people have strong negative opinions about the journey of the soul from its spiritual Home, down to planet Earth, and back again. They often express them quite forcefully: "I don't go in for that kind of speculation," or more humorously, "I'm not coming back as a rabbit!"

Most current reasons given, both for and against the idea of our living a series of lives on Earth, are poorly thought out. That's not at all surprising. People don't read much on the subject—in truth, there's not much good stuff to read, compared with the piles of philosophical and religious literature. There is no agreed authority on the subject to which we may turn, unless we happen to belong to one of the religious groups that teach people about "the wheel of life" or "rebirth"—two alternative expressions frequently used to describe reincarnation. As traditional western religious organizations are opposed to the idea most religious leaders generally ignore it.

Modern concepts about reincarnation have little to do with the historic statements made by Hindus in particular and by some Buddhists. Unless we were raised in these faith traditions, most of us find them difficult to understand and even harder to believe. Jews, Christians, and Muslims have little to go on as, over the years, traditional belief about

1

physical rebirth has been deliberately and even brutally eradicated from these faiths by their leaders.

People do tend to think of reincarnation as a religious doctrine, but it is really more accurately seen as a concept of metaphysics—which is the philosophy of being. Secular thinkers frequently assume that agnosticism or atheism is too solidly grounded in science to permit irrational faith or New Age pronouncements. But science may be ahead of some atheists and even some agnostics. It's our experience that the modern quantum metaphysical concept of reincarnation, when fully explained, finds an acceptance most readily in secular circles.

Our understanding of reincarnation today is grounded not, as some might suppose, in speculation about the occult, but in human knowledge, based on personal discovery and a series of progressive revelations. Observed facts range from established near-death experiences, to the seminal research begun by the late Dr. Ian Stevenson with little children who had memories of a previous human life. There is also the incredibly large body of work, reported since the 1950s, by professional researchers, spearheaded by psychiatrists and psychologists, but including a very substantial number of educated laypeople, who have used hypnotherapy in millions of past-life regressions. Much less socially accepted, the last source of our knowledge is attributed to the few but surprisingly influential top rank psychic channelers.

This book has been written to explore the content of reincarnation concepts, and to clarify their purpose. Since most people have half-baked notions of the matter, basic clarification seems the best course to take for everyone's sake. Skeptics may breathe more easily.

To cover the ground adequately we will employ our experience of channeled speech and writing, originating with senior guides on the Other Side. We are well aware that many readers will not share our conviction that this form of communication is a reality and may be trusted. Neither of the authors is totally naïve, both coming late in life to this experience, but we have spent eight fruitful years constantly working with issues relating to reincarnation.

Toni Ann Winninger is well known at home and abroad as a clear channel psychic, whose principal contact on the Other Side is with a group of senior teachers and spirit guides who call themselves the "Ascended Masters."

Sharing the fruits of this experience, author and master hypnotist Peter Watson Jenkins has sought to provide an opportunity for readers to make their own personal evaluation of reincarnation concepts, based on statements by those on the Other Side who claim a genuine knowledge of the way it works. In this respect they feel that the channeled communications are largely self-authenticating.

In January 2009, at the request of the Masters, we published *The Masters' Reincarnation Handbook, Journey of the Soul.* The little book is a brief but straightforward, no-frills account of the journey of the soul from its celestial "Home" to planet Earth and back again. The setting for this spiritual journey was carefully explained for us by the Masters. The text of their *Handbook* was composed by them on the Other Side, not here on Earth. They dictated the manuscript to Toni, their channel. Translation into English from their vibrational language took place automatically in Toni's subconscious mind; she carefully typed their dictation as the words entered her consciousness.

The next step in the publishing process was that we studied the typescript to assess whether the Masters' claims and comments would be readily understandable. Wherever the translation was at all uncertain we submitted a request to the Masters for clarification. The resulting manuscript was further edited by Peter's wife, Sonia Ness, assuring the correct use of syntax and punctuation. When all our changes had been noted, the revised text was taken back to the

Masters for their final comments. This allowed them to make modifications or additions to the final draft, which they did in a fairly small way. The same careful procedure has been followed for this book.

The Masters regard the *Handbook* as their definitive statement on reincarnation. They intend that it should be used to help souls, incarnated in human form, to understand more fully their nature, and their purpose in being here. The Masters vigorously assert that they have written about the *facts* of our life, and therefore the *Handbook* is never to be seen as a theological or religious construct. They recognize some truth may be found in religion, and they commend the warmth of love to be found in many religious communities, but our freedom as individuals to think things out for ourselves is vitally important to them. They encourage everyone to think freely and not to depend on religious organizations to do their thinking for them. To this end they consistently leave it up to their readers to feel free to assess the value of all the statements they have made—including this present book.

Working with the Masters on several publications, we have come to know them to be a bunch of likeable, happy, fun-loving spirits. They live together in a delightful realm of unconditional love and equality. The spirit world's Home is wholly free from judgment and negativity. To some of us here on planet Earth, Home's atmosphere might seem a little bland without the edge of human rivalry and danger, but it is for them sheer perfection.

This book adds a commentary by Peter to the little *Handbook* to help those who may want a human companion in assessing the meaning of the Masters' words. We have also added a set of seven essays, largely based on the Masters' other writings, to help readers explore selected reincarnation concepts more fully. The topics of these essays cover areas of belief and practice in which the

Masters' viewpoint is distinctively different from current human attitudes. The view from the Other Side, of the "life lessons" that we set up for ourselves before each incarnation, helps to clarify the big issue many people have of identifying their true purpose in being on planet Earth.

So that it may be fully understood that our discussion of the topics of abortion, heaven and hell, homosexuality, suicide, life lessons, and God belief, represents the celestial viewpoint, we have quoted extensively from the Masters' books. You will find quotes from their blog, from our book *Spirit World Wisdom*, and from interviews that Peter conducted with a number of individual souls for our trilogy *Dialogues with Masters of the Spirit World.* Two essays, on Health and healing, and on Spirit life on the Other Side, were composed specifically for this book.

Overall, if we prove well able to clarify for you what the Masters have written, we shall be very gratified. Don't imagine, however, that you will be told what to think. The truth is too precious to be given that kind of treatment. The Ascended Masters indicate we should not expect to discover absolute truth during our present incarnation. Such an attitude goes well with our exploration here of the metaphysics of reincarnation.

Peter Watson Jenkins
Toni Ann Winninger

Publishers' note:

Suggestions for your further reading about reincarnation are contained at the end of this book.

The publishers, Celestial Voices, Inc., invite you to visit their website: www.CelestialVoicesInc.com

The Masters' blog is at: www.ReincarnationGuide.com.

The website's literature page gives details of books, and the messages page has their answers to questions submitted from all over the world.

The Masters' Facebook page is called: Reincarnation Guide. It features essays and daily comments by the Masters on brief questions submitted by the world-wide audience.

Special Terms Defined

Advisory Council: A group of guides, generally twelve in number, who help a soul choose lessons it wishes to experience. Once the soul returns Home the council helps it to understand what it has learned and to make the best use of the lessons it has learned.

Akashic Records: An energetic library containing records of all knowledge and wisdom gained through the experiences that souls have had on Earth. Each soul has its own record of what has transpired throughout each of its many incarnations. The library contains records of everything undertaken by all souls who have spent time on Earth.

Amorphous: Formless, fluid, nebulous.

Belief Systems: Thoughts and actions, initially received and copied from our parents, religion, and society, structuring our behavior. After gaining an awareness of itself, a soul may rewrite or adapt these received beliefs to comply with its own understanding of reality.

Bicameral: Having two chambers.

Contracts: Voluntary agreements that souls make with each other while at Home to ensure that they will have the right Earth experience to help them learn the physical lessons they desire.

Ego: A function of the physical mind that employs judgment and measures how people perceive themselves. It structures thoughts and actions so the soul can operate in society in such a fashion that it may learn lessons and gain wisdom.

Essence: The reality of who a soul is—an eternal part of Source.

Freedom of Choice: A universal law that says all souls have the ultimate right to decide exactly what they are going to do while incarnate. It extends to all aspects of living, from the choice of biological parents, to the lessons souls will learn, how each lesson is played out during their time on Earth, and the manner and time of their physical death.

Home: Not a physical place but rather an energetic dimension of unconditional love and of conscious connection with Source. It is where each soul works with its guides, and council. Every soul not currently incarnating on Earth or in some other place is consciously within the dimension of Home.

Incarnate: A soul who has gone down to planet Earth to gain knowledge and is now in a physical body.

Judgment: A state of mind existing only in Earth's physical dimension. Because of the duality and the polarity of planet Earth, everything has an opposite. Human beings grade all other people by an impression of where the others exist on a personal, ethical, or religious scale of "good" or "bad."

Karma: A term that relates to the effects of an action taken by human beings. Many people use it to explain away what they consider as bad experiences that happen to them. This is inaccurate in its application to human experience. The accurate view is solely the energetic effect of the previous action taken.

Knowledge: Awareness of facts and principles but not necessarily how to use or apply them to life.

Life Lessons: Various experiences on Earth that a soul has pre-planned, which allow it to gain knowledge and wisdom.

Reincarnation: The process the soul uses to experience lessons to obtain wisdom. After completing one physical incarnation, the soul returns Home to assess its experiences and to determine what else it wishes to learn. It then reincarnates by entering into a new physical body in order to have further experiences.

Souls: Individualized pieces of energy split off by and from Source, in order to have unique experiences outside of the perfect. Souls are all particles of Source, so each one is also Source. All souls are equal regardless of the human shell they may have chosen to inhabit.

Soul Group: Those souls who came into being at about the same moment. The group usually numbers 144 souls.

Soul Mates: Members of your soul group with whom you repeatedly incarnate, and with whom you make your most important contracts. Usually the same 18 to 24 souls.

Source: The point of origin of all that is known by human beings, and all that exists. It is the energy of unconditional love, the highest vibrational energy anywhere, and is found in everything. Source makes no judgments and does not reward or punish souls.

Twin Flame: The very last soul from which a soul is separated when individualization from Source occurs.

Universe: For humans the whole creation visible to our optical systems, including the celestial bodies and all the space in between the solid masses. To Source and souls it includes all that exists, whether physical in appearance or purely energetic.

Wisdom: An awareness of the facts and principles of spiritual life together with the understanding of how to apply them in living.

Please note how we use type in this book:

The text of the Masters' Handbook is in bold italic type.

The Editor's commentary on the Handbook is in roman type. So are his words and the quotations from the Masters and various souls that you will find in the essays.

The Editor's questions in the essays are in italic type.

I: Source And Souls

Source

There is in existence an infinite sentient presence which is all-powerful, all-knowing, possesses limitless creative power, and is present everywhere. To help you understand we shall simply call this presence "Source."
Source has no constant form that can be perceived but is an energy that is amorphous and that permeates everything. Its all-powerful essence is one of unconditional love and perfection.

The most difficult part of the entire handbook is at the very beginning. The issue concerns the nature of the Creator. The first comment we need to make is that what is called "Source" does not mean "God," even though that is what the Masters' statements seem to imply at first sight.

Those who understand the theological terms *omnipotent* (all-powerful), *omniscient* (all-knowing), and *omnipresent* (present everywhere), might well expect the sentient creative force in question to be called "God." Instead the name "Source" is given by the Masters, and this may be rather baffling. When the Masters were dictating this book to Toni they insisted that we should never use the *personal* pronoun ("who") when referring to Source. Truly, Source should not be called "The" Source either, and we believe that, were it not for convenience, we would best write "source," without a capital "S," because we are not writing about a person but about *energy*.

Source energy is not similar to the Christian church's third person of the Trinity, because Christians believe that the Holy Spirit is one persona—one face—of a divine triune *person*. God is wholly different—theologians use the words "other than" or "apart from" the soul of man. In our understanding there is no difference between souls and Source: all are entirely Source energy and all are one.

Source cannot be portrayed in the likeness of a being, human or otherwise. The nearest idea for our questing minds, expecting some kind of physical image, is that of a cloud of energy. That idea is present in religious thinking both today and in the past, but this claim is different—Source energy permeates everything. Thus, the central difference between the Masters' view of the Ceator and that of religious orthodoxy is that Source is not "wholly other" than us; it is the energy that is present in every single thing. It is the energy of the entire universe.

At first sight that seems to be fairly straightforward. But in fact the idea is quite radical. It takes us into two areas of debate: (1) the religious controversy about pantheism; and (2) scientific discussion of sub-atomic particles, waves, and strings, and the unified "Theory of Everything." There is the additional issue needing clarification, which comes later, of the relationship of Source and souls.

Pantheism (the original Greek means "God is all") is the belief that god, nature, and the universe are the same. The god of pantheism is not personal, thinking, and creative, but an abstract, blind force. Source is portrayed very differently by the Masters as being not only the essential ingredient of everything that exists, but also a thinking, creative energy of which our souls are fragments. Source energy is soul energy; there is no separate divinity, yet we possess an individuality that informs the whole.

It is when we turn to modern physics that things become rather clearer. Physics is all about energy, an idea that neither religious nor scientific thinkers in past generations defined as clearly as we do today. We need to draw on physics if we are to understand things fully. Einstein identified the entire physical world as being wholly energetic. Energy, which now is measured by physicists as sub-atomic particles or strings, provides the building blocks of our physical reality—our planet, and the great universe of which we are a minuscule part. Everything is energy and there is nothing besides. Paradoxically that is how physics agrees with the Masters' basic premise, assuring us that the Theory of Everything is about dynamic energy, not about static matter. We are talking *quantum* metaphysics, and the old divide in theological thinking—between the two worlds of the spirit and of the flesh—is no longer appropriate.

This dynamic quantum energy is Source. It is the origin of everything, and it permeates everything that exists. Its essence is absolutely positive, creative, feeling and totally accepting. We call its attributes "unconditional love." We may have believed that God created everything, and God is love, and God is in us; but in religion God is set apart from us and always our judge. Source is not set apart but is our essence and is present in every atom within all creation. If you need to think of the infinite, sentient Source, as "divine," then we are all divine. There is no separate divine being controlling the universe and the life of the human soul.

~ * ~

To enrich its knowledge, Source desired to gather information and evaluate all the possible experiences it could ever envision. This work was all contemplated to enable it to comprehend more fully the glory of its own

13

perfection. Relying on its creativity, it developed a way to experience that which was not perfection.

In Source we have a thinking, energetic force that sends itself out, in the form of individual souls, to discover what it does not know about the perfection of its own essence, unconditional love.

When did you last look at yourself in the mirror? What if you had no mirror, no reflecting glass window or crystal pool in which to see yourself? The blind cannot see their face in a mirror—how do they know what they look like? In a burst of rhetoric that sounds a bit like an ancient scripture, the Masters picture Source as sensing something about its "perfection"—but not enough to satisfy its need. The creator of all existence needed to create an energetic mirror by which to assess its own nature—the view from another perspective that can enable a meaningful self-recognition.

Being perfect and unconditionally loving, Source realizes that the only way to achieve an accurate reflected image of itself is by comparison with that which is not the same. We are not talking of physical perfection, but perfection versus imperfection of being. This is the difference between Source's own positive energy and every kind of negative energy imaginable. So Source created negative energy so that it might know and evaluate its qualities more fully.

~ * ~

Source created planet Earth, a world that exists in total duality: everything that exists there also has a polar opposite present. This permits evaluations to be made of every experience souls have while in human form.

14

Planet Earth is the principal tool employed in Source's cosmic experiment. It is a place of absolute duality, a balance carefully maintained between positive elements of love energy and opposing forces of negativity. The Masters have expressed the view that, as creator of everything, Source dwells within the negative as much as within the positive. Negativity is not an unfortunate rebellion by evil-embracing fallen angels against a God of righteousness. It is the more mundane picture of a merchant placing weights on a balance scale. From the soul's perspective nothing is judged as evil—all is experience.

This Source-driven experiment is taking place only on planet Earth because no more experimentation is needed than this one planet affords. There are many other planets used for different life purposes. Planet Earth alone possesses the overall exact balance of negativity and positivity designed for the quest initiated by Source. And so we have the setting for souls to enter the next part of the history lesson.

~ * ~

To start this process, Source split off fragments from itself, which it called souls. The duty of these souls was to enter the Source-created duality to experience the opposite of their own perfection. As each soul's stay upon the planet was completed, both soul and Source would then possess a greater wisdom of the less-than-perfect, and thus would have a better appreciation of the nature of perfection.

The Masters' description of Source's splitting or breaking off fragments of itself neither gives us a clear idea of the process nor reveals anything much about the nature of Source. This activity does not appear to be a birthing. The

Masters insist that all souls are eternally an integral part of Source, despite their having been given independence and unique personality. They affirm that some souls have an impulse to experience duality, which seems logical as they were broken off with that in mind. Those who choose to do so trek down to planet Earth and back again for a long series of lifetimes. These souls, as fragments of Source, experience the opposite of their own perfection, adding to the knowledge of the whole and, by personal reflection, developing their own wisdom.

In the Masters' account of the journey of the soul, all that follows flows in consequence of this plan. It is quite essential to get one aspect of the scene straight, right from the start: *The incarnation of the soul is the means by which Source achieves its fact-finding mission.* The soul is part of Source, so its life is eternal. On Earth, it is like an actor playing a part, to discover what can be made of the character in the play. If we do not get this idea right, we will never understand the reason why awful things happen to us as they do. Understood correctly, we can get a handle on the old human dilemmas of why bad things happen to good people, what the purpose is of pain and negative experience, and why we are here in the first place.

~ * ~

The dimension called "Home"

For the sake of simplicity we will say that Source and all other souls remain in the original energetic dimension from which Source began its evolution. Human beings may wish to refer to this place as "Home." All energy in this spiritual environment has the nature of perfect unconditional love.

16

We may have some difficulty in understanding the phrase "original energetic dimension." Since the word "original" is not described further, we must assume it has to do with a setting that is not measured in terms of the physical universe. That leaves "energetic dimension." A dimension is a measurement. It is not specifically a place. The Masters explain the word in terms of our understanding of radio waves. Broadcasters arbitrarily divide up long, medium, and short radio waves, referring to a broad range of radio frequencies that are measured in millions of wave cycles per second. Like the divisions of wavelengths, divisions of energetic dimensions are broadly based. Earth's "heavy" energy is the Third Dimension; the Fourth Dimension is a fluid interface; and what we call "Home" starts in the Fifth Dimension and goes on from there.

We see our world as space related, so humans often want to know what location (e.g., "up there") the celestial Home may be in. There is no adequate response. After all, every radio wave exists in the same physical location. Home *may* be somewhere, but it's more likely unaffected by space considerations altogether.

There appears to be a purity factor in dimensional gradation—i.e., the higher the dimension, the greater the purity. *"All energy in this spiritual environment has the nature of perfect unconditional love."* Thoughts and feelings are energetic. Loving and positive thoughts are light—fearful and negative thoughts are heavy. In all things that we choose to call "spiritual," energy rules. One interesting little phrase indicates that it was from a perfect environment of purity that Source itself began its own evolution—presumably by breaking off souls. It is a startling thought, however, that the creative force of the universe should also be willing and able to refashion itself. We know of no such parallel in religious thought.

~ * ~

Souls leave Home for planet Earth in order to experience lessons there. They return Home to appreciate, understand, and affirm the wisdom their journeys have afforded them.

The word "wisdom" is important in the Masters' thinking. They make a clear distinction between mere knowledge of something—for example, that some people experience pain—and the deeper understanding that comes through actual personal experience. It is plain that the soul is not merely on a fact-finding mission but on a quest for true first-hand, experienced-based wisdom. Source's own evolution clearly depends on the depth to which individual souls will go in understanding their human experiences.

~ * ~

Each soul leaves a portion of itself at Home at all times. The purpose of remaining partially at Home is to be connected to the whole wisdom of Source, to maintain the flame of love within itself as the soul undertakes further adventures.

The connection is more than just a transmission of Source-energy to maintain the life of the individual soul (although that may be essential because, as we shall see, the soul in turn animates the physical body, which cannot live without soul energy). It is more vital than that. Each soul is a living part of Source the essence of which is in every single one. Though people on Earth may aspire to perfection, individual human beings clearly do not demonstrate it at all times—far from it! The soul is the perfect element in the imperfect human being. We cannot claim that our human personality

18

will always openly reflect unconditional love. On the contrary, there are times when it will not, if we are doing our duty well. More on this paradox later.

~ * ~

Time, space, and the universe

Time, recorded by humans, is peculiar to planet Earth. It is measured by Earth's rotation around the sun, the center of the solar system. Such measurement is meaningless away from Earth since there is no standard by which to evaluate the passage of time in space or on planetary surfaces of varying sizes and at different distances from the sun. This fact creates some difficulty in talking to non-physical spirits about time since they have no point of reference. To them all occurrences exist at the same time. This is useful, however, when people wish to visit a past life to find out about a continuing lesson.

For Toni as a psychic channeler, time issues and requests for her to predict her clients' future can pose a real problem. But what the Masters are saying about time is wholly in line with the findings of modern physics. Indeed, as a hypnotist, Peter sometimes plays a little time game. In response to their request he may take clients to one or two past lives, ending each with their death and return Home. The past lives in question may have been several hundred years ago (by Earth time), but when, after their death, he has returned his clients to the Other Side, he knows they are back in the "Now" where there is no time. So then he is able to help them experience when they planned their present life on Earth with their spirit guides. Thus in a past-life regression session we can have a direct experience of this time issue.

~ * ~

To human minds "universe" is a term encompassing the whole creation visible to human optical systems, including all the celestial bodies and the space in between these solid masses. To Source and all souls the term includes everything that exists, whether physical or energetic.

Within the universe, as perceived by human beings, there are a number of other planets which also have souls experiencing different types of lessons. None of these planets duplicates Earth's energetic duality. Some of the non-human souls are contained in body shells that appear similar to the human body, some are different, and some souls maintain their energetic formlessness without containment.

The Masters point out the differences between our view of the universe and theirs. Our view encompasses only the material world of our third-dimensional planet, and the physical universe into which we snoop with spacecraft and telescopes. The spirit world's multi-dimensional universe incorporates the whole of the energetic creation.

It's probably good for us to acknowledge frankly our very rudimentary understanding of the universe. The Masters fill in the gaps a little for us with their brief description of other planets, which serve souls in different ways and provide other kinds of life lessons. Some planets are inhabited with people of a physical appearance unlike our own—E.T. comes to mind! What they say is that none of these other worlds in any way duplicates the Earth's harsh duality between positive and negative. This is a feature of our planet alone. So it's probably fair to comment that the popular attitude toward aliens from outer space is probably the reverse of the truth—and we human beings are really the frightening ones! More later about that.

~ * ~

The purpose of the soul

The creation of individual souls took place when Source broke off parts of itself in order to be able to have experiences which were then outside that unconditional love of which it was composed and in which it existed.

Souls maintain all of the glory of the Source from which they arose and to which they remain energetically connected. Those who choose to come to Earth to experience duality, where everything has an opposite, initially enter the Earth plane with amnesia concerning this duality, their mission, and their personal past.

The Masters hammer home the theme song of incarnation: It is created by the will of Source that souls may travel beyond their dimensional world, taking with them the radiance of the Creator, Souce, to which they remain fully connected. Then comes the first hint of an important spiritual principle: *"Those who choose to come to Earth."* So while some souls may feel a general duty to do so, there is no compulsion for us to incarnate on planet Earth. We are free to do what we like.

Talking with the 85 souls for our first four books of dialogues, and while working with clients in their between-life regression, we have asked and have been assured that there is total freedom permitted to each soul *not* to incarnate. From what the Masters have said, there is a substantial group of spiritual beings who never have taken human flesh, although they may have incarnated elsewhere.

Then comes the important point about the amnesia given to incarnating souls: Being rendered forgetful, we don't sense the duality of planet Earth between positive and negative; we don't know why we are here; we know nothing about our life at Home or any of the previous human lives we may have lived. This is not a matter of principle but of convenience; in general it is better for us not to know— until we are ready. And some people learn rather more as their life experiences multiply.

~ * ~

Full recollection of the particular experiences of each soul is kept in a recorded volume called its akashic record. Whenever the soul is at Home it has instant recall of all these entries. While human it is in a fog of forgetfulness obscuring all its previously gathered wisdom. During that soul's physical life it may clear enough of the fog from its memory to enable it to recall sections of its past which can help it with its present life.

Our forgetfulness has many variables. The Masters start off by making sure we understand the spiritual norm. Souls at Home are fully aware of everything. Their individual record is kept in a database (remember, everything is energy) known to us on Earth as the akashic record ("*akasha*" is a Sanskrit word for "celestial"). All knowledge gathered by souls on Earth, and the wisdom they have derived from their experiences, is available to all. Amnesia is a practical matter; memory is taken away to save souls on the plane from bypassing the lessons they have set up for themselves and thus rendering the trip to Earth a waste of energy.

But there are exceptions to this amnesia. The late Dr. Ian Stevenson of the University of Virginia explained them with his careful analysis in case studies of little children. As infants we may have had some recollection of being alive previously as someone else. Recollection of a different, practical kind, coming in the form of a specific skill, is not rare—most commonly cited is the musical genius of Mozart. Then there are some individuals who claim to have had a spontaneous knowledge of past lives; the American general George Patton was a case in point. So there is not a complete veil on all memory, and certainly not on physical skills which have often been found through past-life regression to have been passed down from one life to a subsequent one, though not necessarily the very next incarnation.

The Masters allow that we may also try to clear away the fog of amnesia ourselves. That's all right so long as we don't spoil our life lessons by knowing all the answers in advance. Having said that, we are a little surprised that our guides did not write in the *Handbook* what they have told us more than once: that at this moment in human history the energetic shield around the Earth, which causes amnesia to fall over us, is being made easier for us to lift, so that we may have a greater knowledge of who we are and where we have come from.

~ * ~

Because the soul needs a duality to evaluate any experience to know its worth, it can only add knowledge to the compiled wisdom of self and Source while incarnate in a physical body. Further, the experience becomes joint wisdom only when all aspects have been dissected within the polarity, and the purpose for each action and the result of each is completely understood.

Everything we experience, in each part of every day, is an aspect of our many life lessons. We have come from Home (which is devoid of judgment) into a big bad world that is replete with people's judgment of right and wrong, good and bad, pleasant and vile. We make use of this duality to grasp the nature of the positive and the negative—that is why we are here. So the duality may be uncomfortable, but it is essential for our mature understanding. That is the reason we have amnesia until we have largely learned our lessons.

The experience of our life lessons leads us toward an inner wisdom that is more than mere knowledge of a situation. The working out of our choice to take part in the mission from Source to bring back such wisdom is central to our coming to planet Earth.

~ * ~

The reason for incarnation

While the soul is present at Home, it is in unconditional love. No negativity whatever creeps into any facet of that existence. In order to understand how wonderful that state of unconditional love truly is, the soul has to experience being without it.

While at Home, the soul and Source are composed of amorphous energy which swirls around, comingling and sharing in the beautiful energy in which all exist. In order to feel any negativity or lessening of that fantastic energy, a soul must have a physical body. A body provides the nerves and emotions for the sensation of negativity or loss to be felt.

There are many types of negativity, or the absence of unconditional love. First come the strong emotions of the human psyche. The many possible mental and emotional incidents all provide separate life lessons. An incarnate soul may choose to experience anger, hatred, betrayal, worthlessness, self-negation. Other negative

24

experiences may be physical, possibly including cancer, broken bones, and torture. For all of these to be perceived a physical body is absolutely necessary.

The Masters paint a word picture of souls as swirling cloud-like masses of energy. Digital photographs have sometimes come up with surprising additions of bright orbs, big and small. These images, which have often been taken in poor lighting conditions, show air disturbances caused by the energy of visiting spiritual beings.

The soul needs strong human emotions by which it may register its experience of negativity and the absence of unconditional love. The human body provides the physical reactions the soul cannot feel for itself. It is an absolute necessity for us to have a body; without one we could not register either the absence of love or the presence of negativity. In a sense, our body is part of the negativity: it is fragile and self-absorbed, and, being mortal, it eventually dies. The watching souls, appearing sometimes to us as orbs, cannot feel negativity, have no physical limitations or needs, and are eternally part of Source energy.

~ * ~

Planet Earth and other places

In Source's search for a place to have souls experience a variety of emotional trials, it decided to create a classroom where the lessons could be intensified. This would be a location of absolute duality where nothing exists in a vacuum but all energies would have a diametrically opposed force. The school was planet Earth, whose energy then became polarized. Earth is unique. No other place in our perceptible physical universe was created as a duality.

25

Other places were created for souls to have physical encounters, but all these places were dedicated to single intensified experiences: conflicts; various forms of communication such as music, shape, color, vibrations, thought transference; studies concerning physical conditioning and mental ingenuity. In other places areas are reserved for the discussion of intellectual and philosophical matters. In some of these locations the Soul does not need a physical body at all but rather whatever form or shape will permit an evaluation of the lesson being reviewed.

The carefully balanced duality on Earth between positive and negative is unlike any other created environment. Historic human accounts give to God the ultimate upper hand in "the battle between good and evil." In the Masters' account, planet Earth is a classroom in which negative forces are needed as a tool for lesson-learning, and are truly part of the creation. There are no *fallen* angels who say with Satan in Milton's poem *Paradise Lost,* "Evil be thou my good." On the contrary, negative energies are placed in the physical third dimension for the purpose of providing balance, and souls choose to take on negative roles, as we discovered in our startling interview with the soul of Adolf Hitler in *Talking with Leaders of the Past.*

One of the aspects of reincarnation that puzzles most people is that what we call "good" and "evil" are solely Earth-based phenomena. Why can't souls experience evil when they are at Home? The Masters use a classroom analogy in which the loving soul is provided with a whole variety of learning experiences, the most challenging of which is that of understanding the difference between positive and negative energy. The answer to my question is that, were it possible to make this assessment at Home, the atmosphere there would no longer be wholly unconditional,

26

non-judgmental love. *Knowledge* of duality is quite possible in the fifth dimension's loving atmosphere, of course, but actual *experience* of it would drag the soul down to the third dimension. So the judgment of what is "good" and "evil" remains firmly locked as an expression of purely human ethics in the duality of planet Earth.

~ * ~

Nurturing the soul's growth

All souls have a theoretical knowledge of everything, but they will not have the total wisdom of a subject until they have tasted of it themselves. This is the reason that souls continue to reincarnate, coming back to Earth time and again.

Here is one example of this principle: People see astronauts fly into space, walk around in zero gravity, tethered to the space station, bounce on the surface of the moon, and endure the pressures of takeoff and landing. If the observers haven't actually done this work themselves, they can only imagine what stresses are endured by the body, what emotions are generated in the mind—and what relief returning to safety feels like. The wisdom of the event can exist only for those actually taking part.

The Masters feel it is essential to distinguish clearly between knowledge and wisdom. At Home, their shared energetic database makes knowledge readily available to all, as people for whom Toni has channeled information have readily found out. Information about people and events, which can be verified as absolutely correct, is knowledge. Wisdom is more than that and goes deeper than the mere facts. It is experience that has been thoughtfully digested. It is not so much mere knowing but inner certainty that is acquired firsthand, and for which we came down to Earth. It is our unique wisdom, gathered here, that is our soul's contribution to Source's search for understanding.

~ * ~

Souls who are fresh from the warmth of unconditional love start out with simple tasks—to find out what each of the major emotions feels like in a body. Then they will move on to major projects with more complicated scenarios. Each incarnation nourishes personal growth, knowledge, and understanding. Life lessons become more complex, and an individual soul may finish its cycle of incarnations by searching for the true meaning of love and bringing the sensation of unconditional love into the physical body.

As a soul's personal growth during its incarnation approaches its fulfillment, it awakens to its own essence, recalling some of its wisdom gained in previous lives. Then, having a measure of self-awareness, it will generally choose to reach out and assist fellow souls who are struggling to awaken.

There are two growth cycles in the overall wheel of life. First, within each life there is a natural progression by which we take on evermore complex lessons. Sometimes our most difficult lesson is presented to us at birth. In our interviews with the souls of Helen Keller (deaf-blind) and Wilma Rudolph (polio) in *Talking with Twentieth-Century Women*, this tough early start was well illustrated. Sometimes there is a progression of life lessons of varying intensity. For some older souls there may be a letup as the lessons in their human life come to an end and they have a breathing space in which to become more aware of who they truly are as a soul. Newer souls with less experience rarely get through the lessons they came down to learn the first time they attempt them.

The second growth cycle happens over the human centuries during which we are incarnating, going Home, and then reincarnating. People talk a great amount of nonsense about their being "old" souls, as if this were a status symbol. Our response to them should be that all souls are equal, all being particles of Source, and anyway, it is clear that some souls progress more slowly than others, so age is not a useful measurement. Soul growth comes incrementally, one life-lesson experience at a time. When we have mastered the simple tasks, they are not repeated, and we go on to greater challenges. In the end we use our skills to be the guides of other souls who are still struggling to make sense of it all.

~ * ~

The advisory council

Each soul chooses what to do and what to learn during its time on planet Earth. This selection, made both at Home and on Earth, involves the soul's ability to exercise its freedom of choice. The soul does not have to make its pre-choices in a vacuum. Each individual soul has an advisory council, almost always 12 in number, which offers it assistance. The council is composed of colleagues who agree to help the individual soul research how it would like to focus its experiences, and what preparations are necessary for success. These souls may be close friends, or from the same soul group as the soul who is making the journey, or specialists in a specific subject area that the incarnating soul wishes to experience.

Once the soul has dropped into a body, the council does not actively interfere with any aspect of the physical life but watches and waits for requests for help.

29

Within the overall pattern of the individual soul's choosing life lessons, there is collegiality—plenty of people to advise the soul: guides, old friends, and soul mates—and it has complete freedom to choose its own path. The phrase "freedom of choice" is a major celestial law. Even when we get down to the planet we still retain complete freedom to choose our own path. The reason is plain: We would not learn for ourselves if we were told what to do in every circumstance. We saw the same principle in the discussion of amnesia: Free choice gives us integrity in making and fulfilling our decisions, and it means we always retain focus on our goal.

There is a long-running debate in theological circles on predestination versus free will. Both are present here in this situation. Souls were broken off by Source for a purpose and therefore can be said to be predestined to fulfill that task. But in deciding how to do it, souls are free to come down here or not; to take things fast or slowly; to make specific choices of lessons, family, gender, and so on. Yet, having freely made all those choices, the integrity of the soul directs it to fulfill its choice of lessons at some point in its reincarnation cycle, even though it may fail to accomplish all its chosen tasks during a specific lifetime. The absence of interference from the soul's council aids this freedom, but help in the form of advice is still only a request away.

~ * ~

The soul group

When Source began breaking off pieces of itself to make individual souls, those who came into being at about the same moment made plans to help each other with the life lessons they knew they wanted to have. Souls generally ask for assistance from their soul group, those closest to them in point of origin. A strong interconnectedness binds the soul group, which may number as many as 144 individuals.

Souls make important contracts with members of this group because they know them best and they feel most able to depend on them when their presence is needed. Generally, group members have about the same number of incarnations and are similarly advanced and at an equivalent level of wisdom.

People make a big deal out of the idea of belonging to the same soul group as someone else. Most of us have had classroom or sporting team experience and we understand bonding together. In the vast crowd of souls in the universe we do need companions. Thus we work frequently on Earth with a small number of soul mates drawn from the same experience group. From necessity, we are always in contact with other souls. Surprisingly, even a large human family may not include any of our soul mates. We often marry someone from outside the group. Where soul mates help most is in facilitating the specific life lessons we have chosen for ourselves—and, vice versa, we help them with theirs.

The Masters introduce the important word "contracts" into their account. This is a vital matter because it lies at the heart of our need to have soul mates. They give help to enable most of our biggest life lessons to happen. They are the bullying husband, or the woman who steals away with our spouse. They lead us into trouble, or acquaint us with disaster and death. After all, since we are here on the planet to experience negativity, who can be more trusted than our soul mates to give us what we are asking for? I do not mean that soul mates may not also work together for loving, peaceful, progressive ends. Of course they do, and we often recognize them as someone special in our lives, but specific contracts are to help us learn our lessons.

31

~ * ~

Soul mates and twin flames

Soul mates are those other members from the group with whom souls repeatedly incarnate, and on whom they rely for their most vital learning contracts. For example, if a soul wants to experience being totally dependent during a lifetime, it can contract with a soul mate to be a drunken driver who runs it over and turns it into a paraplegic.

Each soul has between 18 and 24 soul mates with whom it works time after time. It is not unusual for a person to have feelings for a soul mate even the first time they meet in an Earthly lifetime. It is almost as if they have known each other for their whole life. They may even find they share dreams or memories in common.

A twin flame is the other half of the last division each soul has from Source. Consider Siamese twins who have been separated. For a period during their early life they did everything as one person. Once separated, they reach out for the one who was once a part of them.

Joining with a twin flame completes that entity, and whenever that takes place nothing else seems to matter to them! When (as happens quite rarely) twin flames do get together during a lifetime, sparks will fly, providing both are at the same level of awareness. If ever twin flames become romantically entwined it is like being back Home. They share the wisdom of the ages in an aura of unconditional love.

It is not always wise for a soul to plan to meet its twin flame on Earth because then it will not want to learn any lessons but simply share physical pleasures with its twin. It is not unusual for twin flames to cut themselves off from family, friends, or even the rest of the world to be together. Both pieces of a "flame" may not be on Earth at the same time.

Human beings are suckers for romantic love, either as participants or as voyeurs. The Masters spend a lot of time on the twin flame issue, which excites a great deal of popular attention. The idea that there is someone "out there" who is perfectly the other half of ourselves is powerful news indeed. But twin flames rarely meet on planet Earth. The Masters say it is not at all common for us to match up with our twin, and whenever that happens it can be quite distracting for us, drawing us away from our carefully planned life lessons. At least if we don't meet our twin flame in this incarnation, we all have the indelible idea that there is someone who is absolutely perfect for us. We are right. There is someone, somewhere out there, waiting for consummation with us. One day. Perhaps this is why the universal human feeling of aloneness is so commonplace. We really do know what it is like to be in a complete whole.

~ * ~

Exploring Reincarnation

II: *From Home to Earth*

Freedom of choice

Once it is decided that a soul is going to have an experience on Earth, the first and foremost universal law comes into play—the soul's freedom of choice. Everything that happens to the soul at any stage of its existence, whether physical or non-physical, is determined by that soul's own choice.

All that happens in every second of the day on Earth is not predetermined, but the desired major life lessons are decided well in advance. For instance, if a soul wants to experience being fully dependent upon another, it may achieve that state by being born malformed, or by becoming an invalid, or by being the property of another. The final decision how this will happen may not come until the life is in progress, and may even change along the way if a soul decides to try the experience in another manner.

The pattern of how a soul's life is lived is determined by its freedom of choice. It begins with making the choice of the human belief systems to follow in daily life, and extends through choice of employment, spouse, and even when it is time to return Home.

We had an enlightening discussion with the soul of Carl Jung, the psychologist, that was reported in our book *Talking with Leaders of the Past.* He told us that we are the

35

creators of our reality, and when we need to experience something we establish the energy that says, "Come to me so I may experience this." He went on to say, "The spirits cannot do anything that the person does not ask for in some way, shape, or form."

As individuals, we tend to flip between the extremes of thinking on the one hand that everything that happens in each moment of the day is wholly within our control or on the other hand that we are totally programmed. As Jung's comment clarifies, the truth lies somewhere in between. We have freely chosen our painful life lessons, but we are never forced to do them. Things that seem to have a big meaning for us happen in response to *our* initiative, whether on the level of the conscious mind, or as an unconscious request, or at the soul level.

In fact, it is often the case that the mental or physical pain we endure with a scowl results from a free choice made by our soul, even though on the conscious level we hate the experience. Our conscious thoughts are often quite willing to fight off the very experience that we have asked to be given us as a life lesson. Sometimes our mind identifies but rejects our lesson and sometimes it doesn't even have a clue that a life lesson is involved at all.

The primacy of our freedom to choose our own path will not be truly understood until we have properly grasped lesson number one: that we are a soul here on Earth on a mission. We are not our body, nor even our conscious mind, although it often feels that way. So the awful feeling of having no choice in matters usually arises because our choices at the soul level have not been readily understood by our mind, or are unacceptable in our ego-based personal philosophy.

~ * ~

Choosing experiences and contracts

The soul has met with its council and decided what experiences it wants to have; then it seeks to make contracts with other souls to help it to fulfill those desires. It continues by discovering which other souls from the group have planned an incarnation at about the same time and may be in a position to help (being the right age and in the right place). Discussions then begin to establish how they may be able to assist the soul and how that favor may be returned.

Sometimes, when this planning stage begins, incarnating souls discover that some major project is going to take place on Earth. It may be a famine, an epidemic, the creation of a dictatorship, or some other regional or global event that would fit into the soul's lesson plan. The soul decides if participating with the masses will fulfill this requirement. Agreements are then forged with all the souls involved to ensure they will have the desired experiences. These are referred to as contracts.

The way the universe of souls works is truly inspiring. Each soul contributes to a web of helpfulness in which the plans of one soul for its next incarnation are matched with the needs and availability of another. To do this effectively all the souls involved must be on the planet in such a way that they can play a part. Sometimes souls get so caught up with giving practical help to a set of soul mates that they return many times to the same extended family or tribe. This is not the normal mode of incarnation because over many lifetimes we will dwell in a wide variety of locations worldwide. In the final stage before they all incarnate, souls form teams to work together. And our conscious minds will never know.

~ * ~

Negativity as a choice

Looking back through human history most people might say, "I wouldn't want to be a slave or a slave master." However, if a soul wants to experience control in all its aspects, it can learn that lesson by being both the oppressed and the oppressor. Remember, only on Earth can souls have an experience of negativity. At Home all is unconditional love. Negative emotions represent the most dramatic opposite of love that can exist. Sociopathic behavior, such as murder, psychosis, and hate, is uniquely possible on Earth. If a soul incarnates but always chooses to be loving, kind, and good, it might as well stay Home.

It was a big deal when the Masters asked us to interview the soul of Adolf Hitler for our book *Talking with Leaders of the Past.* In part one of the interview, which had the soul acting out the person of the Great Dictator, Toni found channeling quite bruising. Later, when talking to Hitler's amiable soul, we learned that a major soul contract had been created, involving millions of souls, and that a major outbreak of negativity, to be led by Hitler, was deliberately planned to be instructive to all the souls involved and to the millions watching them worldwide.

At first it was very hard to accept that what Hitler's soul said was true, but we understand now. A central theme of incarnation was expressed by this agreement: It is that Source made our planet Earth uniquely tough, so visiting souls might experience life in its most negative form. Therefore, we fulfill our mission from Source by being involved as victims of pain and oppression, as well as by taking our place among the perpetrators of negativity, not once but many times, in ways big and small.

~ * ~

Choice of parents, gender, gifts

Having completed the decisions about whatever life lessons it wants to experience, a soul starts considering the stage setting for the drama. It looks around and decides what type of parents will facilitate its goals, and also considers whether the parents' own journey would benefit from having it as a child. So it makes a contract with them.

Next, what gender will make it easy or difficult to accomplish the soul's plans? (Gender may complicate or facilitate some lessons, such as being female in a male-dominated society, or being homosexual, or bisexual, or transgender.) The soul asks itself if gender is a major or minor aspect of its human life. Decisions are made accordingly.

The soul will also ask if it has any skills developed in prior lives that will not interfere with its learning but will help with some other things in this new life. A soul might bring its music, its communication skills, or even its psychic abilities into play. Being a prodigy can present terrific lessons to learn about emotions, interactions, and dealing with people and their prejudices, but a soul does not want to bring so much forward that it only ends up dealing with past issues and not learning anything new.

Note that even the parents' souls are consulted—everything is painstakingly arranged before incarnation takes place. The gender issue is an important one. Souls are naturally without any gender, and they may choose to experience both human genders in the course of their many incarnations. We gather that some souls have a tendency to prefer one gender over the other, as Peter's client learned in the course of being taken back through her 12 past lives, as recounted in his book *Christy's Journey*. For her, the male lives were always "more trouble" than the female lives.

The other big gender issue is that of homosexuality, bisexuality, and transgender. (See the essay later in the book on homosexuality.) These states of being may be deliberate choices by the soul made before incarnating, or they may be the universe's way of interpreting a life lesson, such as the experience of ambivalence or of rejection by others. This was well illustrated in my interview with James Baldwin's soul in *Talking with Twentieth-Century Men*, where his brutal stepfather was a homophobe (which is another aspect of gender ambivalence). This pre-planning of gender issues suggests that being homosexual is not a choice that was made by the individual's *human* mind, though whether or not people express their homosexuality in public can be considered a social choice as opposed to a biological one.

The prodigy issue, which we looked at earlier, relates to the idea of life lessons. We may choose to have an advanced talent, as did Albert Einstein, in order to have a lesson in social isolation. The display of talent is only one of many settings for negative experiences. We guess that this issue of personal talent may be a little unregulated, and that sometimes we bring across a talent from previous lives, as did several of the leading souls with whom I have spoken. Pablo Picasso comes to mind as his soul claimed that he was formerly an artistic craftsman in Africa. His sense of familiarity with "primitive" art forms did not interfere with his lessons as he was unaware of the connection.

~ * ~

Physical connection with the fetus

When contracts have been made for a soul to become the child of a couple, it may help choose the time of conception. With the conjoining of sperm and egg the soul will connect with a tiny energetic string to the fetus, thereby staking its claim to that particular body.

We come to the process of the soul's physical incarnation, starting with the conception—which souls do pay attention to, booking their place, as it were, by using an energetic attachment. In spirit-aware hypnosis practice, these cords or strings are quite commonplace phenomena. Not only are they the soul's link with the fetus, but they are also often observed to exist between those who are controlling, such as a parent, and the one who is controlled.

~ * ~

Older souls who have been in bodies many times are not always ready to jump right in; they want to say goodbye to their friends who remain at Home, and watch how their new family is getting ready for them. Some younger souls may enter the fetal tissue fairly soon after conception because they wish to experience the entire growth process.

Whenever the soul chooses to fully inhabit the fetus, it must be before the fetus leaves the womb. If a fetus leaves the womb without a soul, it is not energetically viable and cannot sustain life. The soul never enters the fetus after it leaves the womb.

While the fetus is in the womb, its life and growth prior to birth depend on the mother's supply of energy, until such time as the soul who has booked its future habitat in the fetus takes over for its incarnation. A simple principle is involved: All human life is supported by a sustaining influx of energy through the soul.

In the case of younger souls the incarnation may be completed quite early—there is no set time. But souls have commented that it is more difficult to squeeze their energy into a tiny fetus than one that is near to term. Also, it is less confining for the soul to be absent during the long period of quiescent fetal growth, and prolonging its enjoyment of spiritual stimulation with its companions among the current batch of incarnating soul mates.

Medical viability is achieved when the fetus is discerned to have reached an "anatomical threshold" at which its organs can sustain life independently. This is unlikely to be until at least 23 weeks after conception. Soul viability is measured quite differently: it is the moment when the incarnating portion of the eternal soul is downloaded into the little body, usually shortly before its birth.

There has been a continuing dispute among regression specialists about whether the soul enters the baby after birth. This the Masters categorically rule out. A baby born without a soul will be born dead, and it is merely confused infant memories, recalled in hypnotic trance, that have suggested otherwise.

~ * ~

Miscarriage and abortion

This topic is a very emotionally charged issue for many human beings. Before we begin let us say clearly that a soul never dies. Therefore a miscarriage or an abortion is not the killing or death of a fetal soul. It is the cessation of the bundle of cells that was growing as the result of the union of a sperm and egg.

Miscarriages are usually the result of a contract made by the mother and father of the cell bundle to deal with all of the emotional results of losing a baby at an early stage of development or even right up to birth (a stillborn baby). In a very few instances, the soul assigned to a fetus may decide that it is not ready to come to Earth at that time and breaks connection with the fetus, causing it to cease functioning. Remember, the soul always has freedom of choice to do this.

The act of having an abortion is a lesson that some souls wish to experience. All the emotions of selfishness, guilt, regret, disdain, and much more, come flooding in from their self and from their relatives. The woman is in a cauldron of stormy feelings and needs to see the lessons she sought without shutting herself down to the event. When, prior to incarnation, an abortion is arranged as a life event, a soul may not even be assigned to that fetus.

The human problem about abortion, made ten times harder emotionally by Doppler pictures of the unborn fetus in the womb, is that we all have a natural attachment to babies and we make the reasonable assumption that if a baby lives in the womb it constitutes a human life. Our parental instinct is very powerful, and theological doctrine generally—but not universally—instructs us that human life is created at conception.

It is something of a surprise to find that the Masters hold a radically different opinion. They talk about a bundle of cells that have no significance as a human child until empowered by an incarnated eternal soul. They also state that where an abortion is anticipated by the universe in consultation with the souls involved—the mother and sometimes the father—no soul may even be assigned to the fetus, the same being true for miscarriages. The only times a soul is directly involved in the abortion situation are when the incarnating soul changes its mind and leaves the womb (resulting in a natural abortion); or when the mother's soul has second thoughts at the last minute, exercising its freedom of choice; or when some unforeseen incident occurs, in which case the soul will quit the fetus well before the procedure ever takes place.

Talking with the soul of actress Sharon Tate, who was murdered when 8½ months pregnant, I learned that even at that late time, because Sharon's murder was pre-arranged, no soul had ever been assigned to the fetus. In the *Leaders'* and *Women's* books, mentioned above, several souls I interviewed, including Pope John XXIII and Mother Teresa, support what has been written by the Masters. (An essay on abortion comes later in this book.)

Having said all that, abortion is a sad state of affairs and our humanity wants to limit or abolish the need for it. But—once again—we live in a dualistic world, and abortion is a negative life lesson for mothers, fathers, families, and all of us to endure. That is not an excuse, any more than the sex trade is excusable. It is a statement of fact about a world that is designed to provide negative experiences for incarnating souls.

~ * ~

Physical and soul interaction

At no time during the life of a body is the soul one hundred percent encapsulated in the physical shell. A portion of the soul always remains at Home. Part of the non-physical soul also forms what humans call the unconscious mind and we call the higher self.

44

The higher self has many different layers, which all have access to the wisdom that the soul has gained in prior lives (the akashic records). While in physical form, the easiest layers to contact are the levels just above the conscious level of awareness. These levels of awareness can easily be reached during meditation and through hypnosis.

When a soul completes the lessons it has incarnated to learn, it finds it can bring forward wisdom from its higher self to help teach other souls how to experience life and be more in touch with the higher or deeper levels of their own higher selves. This is frequently referred to as "awakening."

There is a great deal of speculation about the structure of the soul, and detailed charts have been constructed purporting to show the layers of the higher self. Religious philosophers, drawing on Plato's concepts, have supposed that there is an "astral body" composed of subtle material existing as an interface between the physical body and the intelligent soul. The Masters talk about levels of awareness starting with the unconscious mind and moving upward.

While it is true that a puzzling situation exists in our distinguishing what is physical (our brain cells) and what is energetic (our loving thoughts), this is less important than knowing that we are able to access the soul through meditation and with hypnosis. Indeed, the Masters' statement that the unconscious mind is part of the higher self does make sense of the common conviction that listening to our intuition, having gut feelings, and following our heart's desire are all ways in which may receive messages from our soul. In our experience some of the forms of energetic therapy, such as the meridian-stimulating Emotional Freedom Technique (EFT), may well provide a means of open-eye hypnosis allowing us to talk back to our higher mind.

Whatever we make of the multi-dimensional soul, it seems better by far to learn how to listen to our higher mind—by trusting our intuition, for example—than to waste time speculating about the unseen attributes of the soul itself. After all, awakening to our loving self is what we must all do in the end. Most of us are riddled with self-doubt and holes in our self-love. The remedy is there in making contact with our eternal soul, whose unconditional love and confidence is Source itself.

~ * ~

Downloading the records

When the soul has chosen to come as a new human being it needs some guidelines to help it on its way. It comes down to Earth with amnesia concerning what it has contracted to learn. Complete recollection would not allow it to experience the lesson—it would just observe.

Some of the guideposts a soul can follow are contained in the contracts it has made. For example, in order to experience addiction, it may have chosen an alcoholic family; or a lesson in sexual ambiguity may have been selected. Both these lessons can be contained in DNA records. As the soul enters the fetus the necessary DNA is downloaded into the fetus for it to have the chosen propensities.

Also contained in the DNA records downloaded into the new body is the residue of lessons not completed in prior lifetimes. Some human belief systems would refer to this as "karma"; we simply see it as not-yet-completed lessons. DNA generates thoughts, fears, propensities, and desires that were extremely strong in a past life, but where the root of the lesson was never reached, the emotion is still charged and firing.

I must admit being surprised when the Masters first spoke to me about our DNA as a depositary of information about our past lives. Deoxyribonucleic acid contains the genetic instructions employed in the function and the development of living organisms, facilitating the long-term storage of genetic information.

The Masters have told us (this is not recognized by bio-scientists) that DNA preserves a veritable instruction manual for the life of the soul, ranging from the details of contracts made for the current life to the details of unresolved issues and uncompleted lessons from past lives. This explains the way in which information is retained. It also explains why, when we are in hypnosis, we can access past-life information so easily: it is held in our own DNA.

The word karma is much less used by the Masters than within some spiritual traditions. Karma is seen as a carry-through of past incomplete life lessons. It is a common experience that souls do not finish their work during a lifetime. In consequence—a word not far removed from the meaning of karma—they will pick up the threads of their unfinished business. (This issue is an important one in the case of suicide, discussed in an essay later in the book.)

~ * ~

Amnesia

The downloaded records do not fill in any of the facts that are concealed by the amnesia. The curtains which the amnesia draws over the contracts and lessons the soul has made may be pulled aside as each one of them is completed. The soul may understand why something has occurred and choose not to repeat it.

On the other hand the soul may complete an action, such as being abused by a spouse, and learn to get out of the situation, but still fail to learn why it happened and therefore get into another spousal abuse situation. This can repeat as many times as necessary until the lesson is completely understood. One lesson may even be carried over into a subsequent lifetime if the lesson never gets understood. Amnesia will keep it hidden until understanding is complete.

With a lesson such as spousal abuse, when the woman appreciates that she does not deserve to be a punching bag, and understands the lesson that she is worthy and equal to her spouse, she walks away and will never have to look back. Any amnesia surrounding similar issues of lack of self-worth and equality will start to clear so that she may see the whole picture around those issues.

Now we are able to visualize how amnesia is created—by energetically blocking the information stream from the DNA. Amnesia is partially and progressively reversed when the soul comes to understand the nature and purpose of a particular life lesson.

The Masters now use what must be their favorite and often-repeated illustration: the sad tale of an abused woman who would not learn her lesson. But whether our lesson is hers or something altogether different, we are reminded that learning lessons is the primary reason we chose to be down here on planet Earth. Lessons typically have two elements. The most obvious is the negative experience itself, but that may well be followed by another, like the woman's second marriage: why did negativity go on happening?

Much of the trouble that human beings get into is caused by their lack of self-love. There may be reasons why we have learned to doubt ourselves. Learning lessons often includes coming to terms with the cause of our distress. Doing so allows us to understand what has befallen us, so we can move on.

Finally, the clarity of understanding comes and we are enabled to love ourselves. At this point, having learned the lesson, we will not have to return to it again, and our former mere knowledge of the situation will deepen to become part of the wisdom of our soul.

~ * ~

How soul lessons are learned

The simple way to explain soul lessons is to say that the soul wishes to have the wisdom concerning an action, emotion, or situation which is other than the unconditional love it experiences by being at Home. At Home, Source and all souls possess the knowledge of what every soul has ever experienced. They do not, however, have the wisdom of the experience unless they have performed, lived through, or been a part of the experience itself.

All souls have knowledge about the Holocaust, for example, but only those souls who took part in one way or another have complete wisdom of the physical, mental, and emotional extremes that the events caused the human body and psyche. In other words, living through an experience is the only way possible to gather wisdom from that experience.

Here comes the limiting factor: for a soul to truly have the full wisdom of a situation it must understand why each party did what it did. This can only be done when the soul reaches inside the body and evaluates the experience with its heart and essence. This is the central experience of the Earth lesson journey.

The Masters forcefully present the issue of our achieving wisdom through personal experiences, because this is precisely why we are here on Earth. Overcoming negative challenges in life, and knowing what they mean is tough, but we need to go back in memory to the starting point of our journey and recollect why we are here.

Human life is designed, like the adolescent Australian Aborigine's walkabout. This is an adolescent rite of passage young men undertake. They journey alone and live in the wilderness for many months. In our spiritual aloneness as human beings we are asked to understand the motives we have had, and grasp the nature of our relationships. This is not in order to give or receive praise or blame, but to understand in depth what has happened and why it happened. Such understanding involves not only the details of things we have done in the past, but also our assessment of why other people in our life did what they did to us. Source is seeking to know the nature of itself, and as fragments of Source we are here to do the work involved in our own small way.

~ * ~

The ego and the soul

The polarity of planet Earth creates a unique thing within the human body which is called the ego and is the Earth-master. It tells people whether they are rich, successful, popular, or playing the game of life as their society wants it played.

The measurement device of the ego is judgment. This calculates right or wrong according to the recognized belief systems of others. Ego takes all decisions out of people's hands and places them in the hands of the society. Everything people do gets judged. Consequently, individuals never ask themselves whether they feel like doing something, but rather want to know what is expected of them.

Our conscious mind is dominated by the ego, say the Masters. Sigmund Freud's hypothesis of the ego was of the "organized realistic part of the psyche." What he called the "super-ego" was "the critical and moralizing function." We believe that the Masters are considering both of these aspects of the ego in this passage.

The point they make is that the conscious mind is not just a part of the human apparatus; it is a judgmental part that has come into being in consequence of the polarizing of planet Earth into positive and negative elements. On behalf of the human mind, the ego decides what is good or bad, accepted or rejected, loved or hated. Ego drives the decisions we make about who we are, how well we are doing, and so on. Most of all, ego makes judgments according to its narrow view of social norms and beliefs. These are the norms of society in which we actually live, whether as the member of a church or of a violent gang.

The ego is all-powerful and works in uneasy tension with the soul. The conscious mind can "over-shout" the soul, the Masters have told us, so that the soul cannot even hear its own counsel. The ego is powerful because it is physical, and the soul, confined within the physical body, is very much affected by the physical. The ego controls the belief systems that the person feels must be obeyed.

~ * ~

When a soul is wholly controlled by its ego it cannot learn soul lessons. This is because the soul is no longer exercising its freedom of choice to gather knowledge; it is merely following the mandate of others. The soul must become aware of its own power. It must recognize its ability, first to make choices, then to evaluate everything that it perceives, and finally to decide if something can be learned from it and whether or not it is something that needs to be repeated.

It might seem strange at first to imagine the soul can be overpowered by the conscious mind. Is not the soul part of the powerful eternal Source? Yes, it is, and that is precisely why the ego can overpower it. Elaborate precautions are taken for souls to have amnesia to avoid interference from past-life memories. In the same way, souls are not given power to coerce the ego to think one way or another, lest that prevent the mental mistakes that are part and parcel of its negative experiences.

So the soul has to reawaken the power of love, which is its essence, and work on the ego with gentle persuasion. Thus the ego may recover its ability to make and carry through unbiased choices that may have little to do with societal norms and religious edicts but represent the right way to go forward.

~ * ~

Facts with which the ego deals come from outside the body. They are put into the brain through the eyes or the ears. These are the spoken and written ideas of other people and are accepted most of the time without question. Knowledge with which the soul deals can be found within. It comes from comparing feelings of past experiences with feelings of unconditional love. To use the soul to learn life lessons one must ask, "What do I feel about this?"—never, "What do I think about this?"

In the bicameral (two chambers) psyche of the human being, one chamber (the ego and super-ego) is intent on listening to other people's advice, and creating judgments based on human learning. Millions of people function on the basis of "what I think"—the promptings of their intuition being largely or wholly ignored. But the other chamber (the soul) is equipped with the knowledge of the universe, expressed in terms of "how I feel." This is the spiritual approach, and the Masters frequently tell us that the more we trust our intuition, the easier it is to make sound decisions, because then our ego is relegated to its proper role: making small decisions about unimportant issues.

~ * ~

Accidents, disease, and old age

Accidents, disease, and old age are all ways for souls to learn lessons. Truly, there is no such thing as an accident because any event engaged in was chosen by the soul to learn something about itself and its lessons. It may be the prelude to a major change in life that finally prompts the questions, "Why did this happen? What did I learn from this situation?"

Disease is best called "dis-ease" because the body, in the soul's view, is out of balance with itself. It gives the soul many opportunities to see the effect of the choices it has made. The body is composed of an energetic life force flowing through a skin-covered container. Everything that humans do affects the flow of energy in one way or another. When people become nervous, the systems of the body go into overdrive causing spasms and extra-acidic conditions. Holding back on emotions or thinking only negative thoughts will shut down the flow of energy. This prevents areas of the body from getting nutrients or causes blockages that interfere with the energy flow. Humans can put any part of their body out of whack by thoughts. Correct the thoughts and the flow resumes.

Old age may be part of a life lesson to go from independence to dependence. The pain, incapacity, or mental confusion in old age may all be a soul's lessons or those that a soul mate wished to experience by being responsible for someone later in life.

If you watch commercially sponsored television in the USA for more than a few hours, you will know what it is like to get depressed. Typical daily fare on "the box" is an advertisement for a drug designed to help eliminate the symptoms of a disease, or even its physical cause. You may not have the disease, but unless you reach for the mute button the script is designed to pull you in and feel sympathetic nervousness. Then the effects of the advertised pill (which usually only masks the symptoms) are further described in terms of so-called "side-effects," which may include serious medical conditions and even death. So a scenario is set up and reinforced many times a night over many months, until we have a low-level of anxiety, or even fear if we identify the disease as one we are experiencing.

Fear (even in the mild form we know as we sit glued to the television), creates imbalance in the human body and mind. In other writings the Masters describe how people who think they may be susceptible to cancer make themselves vulnerable to the disease simply through their negative thoughts. But while a doctor's negative prognosis may accelerate the onset of disease or death, a positive, hopeful attitude expressed by a physician may help the patient to recover—sometimes from the worst of ailments.

In this we see the positive contribution the soul can make to balance the body and to promote healing.

As the Masters point out, dis-ease, pain, dependence on other people, physical incapacity, and mental confusion are all part of the varied provision made by the universe to give us life lessons. There are no accidents. Everything happens for our ultimate benefit in having lessons to learn.

~ * ~

Heaven and hell

Home is a place of continuous unconditional love. Duality exists only on planet Earth. The concept of heaven and hell is of polar opposites and exists only on Earth.

Many religious organizations use the idea of heaven and hell as a reward or a punishment for following or not following their own rules and regulations. This is an invention of the ego, which wants to make judgments on all activities. It is a means of controlling people who are told, "Do as we say or suffer the consequences."

Heaven exists on Earth in the form of happiness, familial love, and sharing and caring between people. Hell exists on Earth in the form of oppression, murder, and abuse. A soul can also create a hell it may feel it deserves, such as cancer.

Once the soul leaves the body it enters a state of unconditional love, void of any judgment concerning its actions on Earth connected with the lessons it decided to experience in that life. There's nothing to be condemned or rewarded.

People may sense that the Masters are opposed to the activities and teaching of religious organizations. On the contrary, they readily acknowledge value in religious communities as caring, supportive societies. On the other hand, although they do not make judgments but only broad evaluations, they are concerned about the control that religious leaders exercise over the minds of their followers. This control is unacceptable to them because it inhibits our soul's freedom to choose its own path.

Heaven is not a complete myth, nor is hell. They are real states of mind here on Earth. We can experience heaven in human love, the beauty of nature and art, and the like. Hell is Hitler's death camps, a brutal husband, a controlling mother, and more. These are real states of mind representing the duality of Earth in our lives. The myths of heaven as a place of reward in the afterlife and hell as a place of punishment in the afterlife are both false. The primary reason is the inaccurate view religions hold about God, judgment, and the purpose of the soul.

Source is not a person, wielding power and judgment over his creation. Source is the fundamental energy of the entire universe, and every soul is a complete fragment of that energy. Moreover, in the thinking of the spirit world, those things that human beings brand as good or evil, worthy of praise or blame, are only consequences of the soul's quest for experience. They have no meaning except in the dualistic judgments of human society.

You will find an essay on "Heaven, Hell, and Suicide" later in this book. The issue of God belief is the main topic in the final essay, entitled ""Making Changes."

~ * ~

III: *Transition Home*

Ending the assignment

The soul generally has a built-in time frame for completing its lessons. When its work is done the soul usually returns Home. If the soul has not understood the lesson within the experiences it has just finished, it may choose to take on another example within that same lifetime to see if it can understand it the next time it is presented.

If a soul returns Home before fully understanding all the facets of its task, it will have to return to Earth to do it over again. In some cultures this carry-over is called "karma." This is not a punishment but rather an uncompleted task the soul itself wants to accomplish. It is not unusual for the soul on its return to Earth to bear a physical mark or affliction reminiscent of the activity it came back to complete.

When the soul has finished and has understood all the lessons it came to learn, it may choose to return Home immediately or to use its remaining Earth time to enter into service of other souls. If the soul enters into service, it will help other souls to understand lessons from which it has gained wisdom, lessons the others are in the midst of learning.

That dreadfully misused word "karma" at last! Speaking with the soul of the philosopher William James in a dialogue we had for the *Leaders* book, I suggested that "consequence" was a possible synonym for karma. He said, "The karma that we know about best is from the Eastern philosophies, wherein is stated that the karmic effect determines everything you do in your next lifetime—which is phooey! The consequence flows from the entire experience of the soul's attempting to learn its life lessons in order to attain spiritual wisdom."

An unfinished or misunderstood life lesson may well be reworked by the soul during the same lifetime. But remember the Masters' illustration of the abused spouse's needing to learn self-love? Well, the soul can try again with another spouse, but if it fails in its attempt during that lifetime, then the essence of the lesson will reappear in a subsequent life.

It may come as something of a shock to learn that the soul is free to "pull the plug" on a lifetime and go Home rather than stay around. True, there are options: We can put off our return and help other people, or perhaps deepen our wisdom by contemplation. Yet the end of life is much more in the hands of the soul than our conscious minds would like to believe. Indeed, another factor may be that our death is pre-planned, possibly as a contract made in advance to give other souls experience of grief when sudden loss occurs.

~ * ~

Death

Death is the term humans use to describe the cessation of continued life when the soul leaves the human body-shell it has been using. Just as the fetus is not able to exist as a living, breathing thing without a soul, so also the body ceases to function when the soul leaves.

There may be an easy transition for the soul who returns Home immediately. Or a soul may be confused and not totally aware that it is able to go Home, so it may roam around for a while, trying to maintain contact with the living.

Human beings see death as done to them, but in a sense it is the soul who initiates death. There are no accidents. The car crash, death from cancer, even murder, may be one of several possibilities: a life lesson, a contract being worked out, part of a larger lesson for many souls, a timely ending, or just a decision made by a soul who has had enough.

The manner of death is not the only issue for the soul. Many older people have become weak, and the soul is having trouble shaking off the Earthly experience that now is weighing it down and clouding a clear transition back Home. Confusion also often happens in cases of sudden death, where the soul does not realize it is no longer connected to a body.

A very different confusion exists with negative expectations—for example, a soul thinks it will go to hell or be punished for drinking or taking drugs, for committing suicide, or for having an abortion. The result can be a delay of the normal transition made by the vast majority of returning souls. Souls may be lost for a few hours until they come to their senses, or they may even hover around the fourth dimension for centuries. People sometimes see or hear them and call them "ghosts." Some of the souls most negatively influenced choose to cause mischief among the living. These we call poltergeists or demons. Others seek the comfort of a living person and attach themselves to someone, or even to a succession of people.

In the end, lost souls return Home, but that is always because they have come to the realization that it is a better state to be in than their current feeling of being lost.

~ * ~

Suicide

Suicide is a life lesson that may be chosen by the soul. When contracts have been made between soul mates to experience the heartache, trauma, and emotional upset of the swift, unexpected ending of a life, suicide is generally the tool employed.

Another reason for suicide is for an early return Home—the choice of the soul itself. Remember, all souls have freedom of choice. Occasionally, a soul feels completely overwhelmed with its human existence (having bitten off more than it can chew). It wants to call a halt to continued frustration so that it may start over again and do things differently. It will then leave the existing physical life by killing the body in some fashion.

Suicide is not the ultimate sin as some human belief systems teach. Once the soul leaves the body it returns to unconditional love to evaluate what went wrong and how to experience the desired lessons in a more palatable manner. It will eventually come back to fulfill the lessons.

When Peter worked as a stockbroker some clients had complicated trading strategies in the options market. One day he was dealing with a highly complex option spread and his patience ran out. His client had even less knowledge and was of no help. So Peter called the team manager and he took over, letting Peter look over his shoulder as the trade was placed. Suicide is like that in the spirit world—we recognize that we are out of our depth and swim for the nearest rock.

Suicide seems like the abortion issue. In both, human beings have a strong sense of revulsion, but the spirit world does not. The reason is that *we* are afraid of death and loss;

they know that there is no loss involved only missed opportunities. There is no death—you cannot kill the eternal soul.

~ * ~

Divesting attachments

A problem that may arise, when the soul has decided to return Home, is a series of Earth-bound attachments connecting parts of it to incarnate souls still remaining on Earth. As life lessons are studied, aspects of the soul become connected to others. For example, when a soul takes responsibility for another, a thread holding them together forms until cut by one party or the other.

A soul's need to continue supplying its physical child with its energy may become a habit that prevents the soul from being able to let go of the child, pull away, and return Home. This also frequently happens with spouses when one body has reached its exhaustion point but the other refuses to let go.

If a person senses that someone is holding on to life because the two have a connection they no longer need, the person can simply disconnect it, or give the other one permission to do so and return Home.

Release of spiritual attachments from one living person by another is practiced by specialists all over the world. Varieties of spiritual release have been practiced in various ways for many centuries. Sometimes it involves cutting or detaching an energetic cord, or it may go deeper into the fear, anger, hatred, loathing that one person feels about another. We have been privileged to help a number of clients hampered by attachment to a dominant parent, spouse, lover, or even their child. As the Masters point out, attachments may delay the soul's return Home. It is best if release can be made well before death, as this will sometimes be all that is needed to save the soul from struggling to maintain human life in old age or severe illness.

One client whom we remember was a woman who found her mother very dominant and demanding. The client was an intelligent, healthy, strong, 30-something mother with a small boy. At the very end of a hypnosis session, having failed to find any attachment in trance, she opened her eyes and blurted out, "I can see a cord going to my mother." She was taken back into hypnosis where she was able to cut the cord. The next week she reported calling her mother only three times that week, having felt compelled for years to call her four or five times a day.

~ * ~

Choosing to stay

There are a number of reasons why a soul may choose to remain when it is time to return. First there are people who are unaware of what happens at transition and fear that death is final and that they will exist no more, rendering everything they have done in life worthless. They cling with their last ounce of intention to their ailing body. This may be a reason for a soul's body staying in a vegetative state for a period of time.

Some relatives think they are opting out of personal obligations and do not want to leave others in the lurch. They can be told that all will be well, and that they may move on when they are ready. They don't have to struggle to remain; they need only think of themselves at this stage of life. Remaining on Earth helps neither them nor their relatives.

The soul may have decided to leave after a certain period of time but then finds that it has turned the knowledge it gained into wisdom and is now in a position to help others if it sticks around instead of leaving. The soul could choose to remain if it had not already planned for its body to deteriorate to an extent that renders it useless.

The soul may choose to stick around after the point of leaving the body but before completely departing from the heavy energy that surrounds the Earth. It may not be able to accept fully that it died physically, so it stays, trying to communicate further with its loved ones.

Some souls remain out of negative energy, such as hatred or revenge, seeking to get even with whoever may have been involved in their passing. These souls will receive assistance from other souls to realize what is happening to them and that they are stuck between two dimensions, the physical and the non-physical.

Some of those who remain believe that they are needed by other souls still in the body. They stay close to help out, even though they are not physical, and may not even be felt by those they seek to assist. These souls should be counseled to return Home because, once there, they can always watch over and assist those on Earth with all the power of unconditional love.

The Masters paint a very clear picture of the many reasons why souls do not transition or, if they do let the body die, do not move to the higher dimensions but remain in the fourth dimension, between Earth and Home, as "lost" souls. There is no chance that Source will abandon them. Souls are sent to guide them Home, though this may prove a long and tricky situation in which a lost soul has dug a hell hole it imagines it deserves, and refuses to accept the help that is proffered.

If there is a time when traditional religion shows more compassion than the secular world, it is at the celebration of Halloween. The Church loving remembers and prays for the souls of the departed, while the secular society dresses up sometimes quite grotesquely, and makes fun of them, from ghosts to witches, and even, oddly, to Mary Shelly's fictional character Frankenstein. In some areas, masks are worn to hide the owners from ghosts that may be looking for them.

Both sides are mistaken. The church's prayers reflect its doctrine of judgment, heaven, and hell, while the secular Halloween displays people's fear of the unknown, and irrational loathing for souls who have lost their way.

~ * ~

Returning Home

Once the soul is free of the heavy body that has encased it during its time on Earth, it floats into the cloudlike, amorphous energy of unconditional love that is the Home of Source and of all other fragments of Source.

What does the soul perceive? It will depend upon what it wants to see. An older soul is very comfortable in a cloudlike state because it allows itself to be connected with all that exists at the same time. It may also be present in many different places all at once.

A soul having difficulty adjusting to Home after the rigid body it wore on Earth may choose to clothe itself for a while in a body form. It may also be more comfortable seeing all its friends similarly attired, and they will oblige. For a while a younger soul also may believe that the body it wore is an example of its true nature, at least until it finally adapts.

If a soul believes that it has led a bad life it may create whatever it interprets hell to be like, and that is

*where it will find itself. The eternal soul is magnificent
and it can create endless versions of where it wants to be.*

There's a saying: "Angels have wings because they take
themselves lightly." There is no discussion of angels in the
Masters' *Handbook*, but we do get a peep at what life is like
on the Other Side. The caring environment at Home is
evident in the way souls are welcomed and gently eased into
the energetic environment. When we interviewed the soul
of Elvis Presley for *Talking with Twentieth-Century Men*, he
told me that his current occupation was to play and sing for
the souls of little children returning from Earth. Elvis the
man was very fond of kids, so the job is just right for him.

We need to be wary of too much speculation about our
energetic Home. People love to go on long, speculative ego
trips, pretending they know precisely what life is like in the
fifth and higher dimensions. They've got it all mapped out in
their articles, charts, and books. We believe that such flights
of fancy make it harder for the clear message of the Masters
to get through to doubters.

~ * ~

Life review

*Shortly after returning Home the soul meets again with
its council. Their debriefing will include all the soul's
activities during the period it has been away from Home.
They evaluate all its contracts and lessons, and the
service it may have had time to give others.*

*With all this knowledge in hand, the soul tries to
incorporate all the wisdom its experiences made
available. It may take a while (in Earth-time) for
everything to be understood. If any of its lessons were not
completed or understood, it sees, with the assistance of*

its council, what it failed to understand, and makes notes to include that in its next incarnation.

We sometimes call the process "debriefing." Whatever it is called matters less than our understanding that the peer review of the lessons a soul learned in a lifetime is of great importance. From the spirit world's perspective this is the point when the soul may finally come to recognize what has happened to it, and what its experiences all meant. There is plenty of opportunity and help for the soul to digest the information it learns. It goes back through its life, registering not only what it did and said to others but (with deepened spiritual insight) how they felt in return.

Life review is not for other souls to judge us, nor even for us to judge ourselves, but rather for us to evaluate the amount of understanding we gleaned from our time on the planet. The Masters make it abundantly clear that there is no right and wrong to be judged; there is only the need to assess the thoroughness and depth of the life-lesson experiences. It's not terribly easy to grasp fully what the spirit world's review process entails, but we know it is comprehensive.

~ * ~

Living between incarnations

Once the soul has had the opportunity to finish going over its most recent life, it spends time catching up with friends and soul mates, finding out what they have been up to during their Earth journeys. The soul may have become involved in some activity or other on Earth and want to monitor its ongoing development carefully. On return, the soul may even become a guide to assist those souls still engaged in the project.

When younger souls (who have not been to Earth many times) return, they are sometimes confused by all the sensory information that is now available to them. Everything that has been experienced by their companions is available for download. It is not unusual for them to need assistance in handling this information, and advice on what may be done with it. A group of souls is always available to help with this process of integration and acclimation.

Groups of souls who had similar experiences while on Earth, such as having committed suicide, may get together to share their experiences so they may better understand the implications of their own feelings, and the reactions of other people. Some take the position of counselor to aid those experiencing difficulties.

As we have mentioned, the soul can choose its appearance at Home, so there are souls who help with those wishing to remain children for a while longer, and those who feel they deserve their physical disability— until they understand the lesson behind it.

As the soul communicates with those at Home it gets ideas of what it might wish to accomplish next. As it monitors what else is happening on the planet and elsewhere, it seeks to decide what new adventures would increase its wisdom and then starts talking with its council to plan the next journey.

Some people find it disturbing to be told that souls at Home monitor and advise our Earthly lives. The thought that someone may be watching our most intimate moments is capable of freaking us out! Nevertheless, despite assurances that our inner thoughts are rarely monitored, the fact is that guides, former family members, helpers of one kind or another, and the amazing life-force energy are all around to help and sustain us.

One example must suffice. After a bridge across the Mississippi collapsed, a few people died in their cars, but other cars and their occupants survived and a school bus laden with children narrowly escaped a watery death. We asked the Masters about those who died. Their answer was that it was their time to transition so they were on the bridge at that moment. Then we inquired how it was possible that the school bus, full of children, had not toppled over into the water. They said that the spirit world helped energetically by "nudging things a bit," to ensure that nothing would cause the death of the children. We know they were serious in telling us that. It would seem that Jesus was right: "The very hairs of your head are all numbered."

~ * ~

Returning to Source

This is a section that the reader might expect to come along about now. The truth of the matter is that souls are never away from Source. Source energy is everywhere and in everything. Source energy is the very energy of each individual soul. Souls never have to return because they never left.

The Masters were laughing when they dictated this short paragraph to their channel Toni. The passage speaks for itself. Thanks are due to the Masters for communicating the truth about the life of the soul and its journey here on planet Earth. We hope you treasure their words as much as we do.

~ * ~

Summary: Journey of the Soul

Energy

Paradox—an apparent contradiction that may be true—is a word that comes to mind when reading the Masters' description of reincarnation.

At the start of the soul's journey is the "breaking off" from Source of the individual soul and small groups of souls. Being thus separated from Source, souls gain individuality, further enhanced by the ironclad universal law that all souls have freedom to choose their own path. Each soul is then partnered by its soul mates, who work with it in a reciprocal system of helpful contracts.

The paradox in this arrangement is that leaving Source is only one way of looking at things. The soul still remains eternally part of Source, resonating with its energy and returning to contribute all its knowledge to the akashic knowledge bank, adding the wisdom it gained on Earth to the wisdom of the universal whole.

If you, like us, have fed from the bowl of traditional religious thought, this aspect of reincarnation is hard. We are used to the grand stories of human mythology, the vision quest, the walkabout, the desire of the individual to go forth and seek to follow his or her bliss. The rest of the account of our soul's journey is refreshingly like that. But the heart of the journey, from start to finish, is new and, being unfamiliar, is unsettling. It is because belief in God as an almighty, eternal judge, which religions have taught us, gets in the way of the truth about Source energy.

We should add that in no way do the Masters teach a form of pantheism—finding a miniature divinity in every rock and tree. Yet in the dynamic, energetic sense, the essence of what we may choose to call "divinity" truly is in every such place because all energy is the energy of Source, and its energy is in everything, everywhere.

Ethics

Getting rid of the idea of any separation between Creator and creation is the starting point for further puzzlement. The soul's journey is to learn lessons in a bifurcated world, deliberately split by Source in a neat balance of positive and negative energy. When coming to planet Earth the soul may choose to live on either side of the negative experience: the bully or the bullied, Hitler or one of Hitler's victims. The choice has nothing to do with right or wrong in human terms. Ethical systems do not apply to our choice of life because it is the actor's role we have chosen to play.

In a movie or a play we may denounce (or boo) the villain as he slits his victim's throat, but, at the end, we may applaud the actor's skill and award him a prize for his work. Planet Earth's a stage and souls are merely players. They are here to gain knowledge of the positive and negative, and learn to live and die in a world evenly balanced between the two. It is for this reason that heaven and hell are no more than states of mind here on Earth. There is no judgment on the goodness or evil of our lives, because human ethics are human stage directions for the roles we play, and not an analysis of what our souls have done. No judgment means there is neither heavenly reward nor hellish punishment. Souls go Home after each lifetime, just as actors go home after each performance of a play.

There may be no judgment, as human religion and ethics would like to have it, but there is self-evaluation made by each returning soul, aided by its council of a dozen peers. This is because the soul has set itself up to learn lessons, and to fulfill contracts made with other souls. Just as human actors sometimes perform poorly, so incarnate souls may be distracted, allow the human ego to overpower their sense of purpose, or take on more challenges than they can manage. There is a delicate balance to this evaluation: it isn't criticism because all is done in unconditional love. The goal is to complete lessons, and this self-evaluation is what is looked for in the review.

The Masters' purpose

The Masters' purpose in providing us with this book is one of achieving clarity. They are sympathetic with the difficulty some people on Earth may have in believing a book claiming to have been dictated by a bunch of spirit guides on the Other Side to a human psychic channel. The Masters are also gently aware of those whose religious sensitivities and beliefs are challenged or even offended by the explanations made in this book. They assure us they are not trying to score points, nor even to win an argument.

What the Masters are doing, lovingly, is presenting the facts of the wheel of life so, believing or not, you will know what they are. There is no conversion involved, no church, temple, or mosque to join. They just hope you will ask your intuitive self truthfully, "What do I *feel* about all this?"

~ * ~

*This is the conclusion of the Commentary on the Masters'
Reincarnation Handbook.*

71

Exploring Reincarnation

Introducing the Essays

The following essays pick up several of the important issues raised by the Masters, as well as two new topical subjects, "Health and Healing" and "Life Lessons." These deserve special notice as they are important issues in our thinking about the purpose of our soul's coming down to the duality of planet Earth. In another guise, it's the long-debated theological issue "Why do bad things happen to good people?" that causes so many teachers of the leading religions to be tied in epistemological knots. Known also as "the problem of evil," this issue is always a tough one for anybody to discuss, but reincarnation shows it clearly and logically connected to the basic purpose of our being here.

There was another topic that we discussed. We called the essay "Spirit life on the Other Side," but in fact it turned out to be a fairly broad discussion, and provided answers to questions we had always wanted to ask but had never got round to before.

In order to flesh out points made by the Masters on their Internet blog and in their *Handbook*, we include exchanges from our interviews of 82 souls, contained in our books. We find the personal details supplied by individual souls most refreshing and very helpful.

The Masters say of themselves that most of them have completed their incarnation cycles, and now they work together as a group of friends, teaching and advising other souls. When asking them questions, Toni has often reported that they stop to have a group discussion prior to giving an answer. Not so individual souls with whom we have spoken. While they are consciously benefitting from the fifth dimension's calm and loving atmosphere of unconditional love, they manage to express themselves as individuals, with distinctive points of view. We feel that reference to what they had to say brings freshness and nuanced minor variations from the Masters' carefully discussed and painstakingly agreed viewpoint.

The topics of our other essays truly picked themselves. With sharp differences in human society over abortion and homosexuality, and the teaching of religion about heaven, hell, and suicide, these were topics that just had to be explored.

From conversation with many spiritual enquirers, we know that there is much confusion about the issue of life lessons and soul contracts, chosen and agreed before our incarnation. Experience also shows that people are greatly interested in the issue of healing. For this specific subject the Masters dictated the whole essay. To develop our theme in the "Life Lessons" essay, we leaned hard on our record of what individual souls have told us.

Abortion

An acrid public debate

There are few issues as dire as abortion for raising people's temperature. Families are split in two over the issue; parents fall out with children; old friends stop talking with each other. We even use different descriptions to describe our attitudes: "pro-life" and "anti-abortion" versus "pro-choice" and "pro-abortion." (The last description is a term of abuse levied by pro-lifers on their opponents—who actually view abortion as a regrettable but necessary evil.)

We are not writing this to join in the acrid debate on its present terms. We suggest grounds for a new viewpoint on the matter, recognizing the heartfelt anguish of all people who seriously consider abortion, and the conflicting views many people have about women who have felt it necessary to resort to abortion. At this point, I want to give you—in the phrase credited to that successful old police drama *Dragnet*—"just the facts, ma'am." We've had quite enough of the battle.

The Masters helped us to organize books of interviews with the souls of people, some well-known and others little-known, who walked on this Earth quite recently. In this essay we refer to three books of interviews that we have published. These are: *The Masters' Reincarnation Handbook* that is printed in this volume (abve); *Talking with Leaders of the Past;* and *Talking with Twentieth-Century Women.* This

75

has given us the opportunity to hear from individual souls their thoughts on the topic of abortion.

First, a view from the trenches. We start our discussion with the souls of three celebrities who were able to speak both from their personal experience of abortion and from their spirit-eye overview of the whole issue.

Marilyn Monroe

This verbal exchange took place during our interview of Marilyn. It paints a very sad picture. When, finally, the film star married the playwright Arthur Miller, whom she really loved, her past abortions caught up with her:

"During your marriage you had an unhappy ectopic pregnancy followed by another miscarriage. It is also said that during your lifetime you had a dozen abortions. Can you tell us about these aspects of your life as you see it now?"

"Well it wasn't a dozen. There were many, but it was not a dozen. I was experiencing in my lifetime as Marilyn Monroe a myriad of emotions—beginning with the sense of worthlessness that I felt as a child, which came out as the callousness with which I treated other lives. When it came to fetuses (particularly early on in my career) I never wanted to subject another little being to what I had gone through, but easy birth control was not readily available in society at that time, making things very difficult and resulting in several unwanted pregnancies. I saw it as wrecking my career were I to have a child. So whenever the situation arose that the result of my encounters was a pregnancy, I could not and would not let the child come into the world—that is until I was with Arthur [Miller]. With him I felt more of a whole person than with anyone else. He had accepted the whole package, which included my mind. I would have loved to have been able to present him with a child. A child of ours would have been extraordinary, but because of my previous terminations, my body was not physically able to carry a fetus to term."

Carmen Miranda

Reading the next extract, remember that Carmen, who was also something of a sex goddess in her time, is answering our questions from the Other Side:

"In 1955, while shooting 'The Jimmy Durante Show,' you collapsed, dying later that night at the age of 46. The autopsy said the cause of death was pre-eclampsia, a heart condition linked with pregnancy. Had your soul decided to die then?"

"My soul recognized that I had experienced all of the lessons that I had come down for, that I was in a pattern where certain things were prevented from being completed because of what I had done to my body and what had been done to my body, so that there was no reason to remain in physical form."

"Were you physically aware of being pregnant?"
"No, I was not."

"Had you ever been pregnant before?"
"Yes."

"And did you have abortions?"
"Yes."

"Tell us about your feeling about abortions."
"The feeling I had at the time of the decision to have the abortion was that it was totally inconvenient for me to bring another being into the world who would compel my attention away from the career that I was embarked upon at

the time. I had totally eschewed the religion of my upbringing, so I did not let that influence my decision. It was done completely on a convenience basis.

"From my position now, I know that these were decisions I made so that I would have the energy of the memory to haunt me—to come back into my thoughts in subsequent periods of time in that lifetime. I know now that the conglomeration of cells within me never contained souls, so there was never another soul involved in the decision, because it was determined that its physical life was never going to get to that point."

"So abortion was not a taking of a soul's life?"

"Certainly not. A soul does not enter into the mix until there is true viability, and even at the physical point where medical people argue there is 'viability' (after a certain number of cellular divisions), the soul chooses when it is going to come in, knowing the pathway that the mother has chosen for herself—that is, whether to go to full term or to terminate."

"So the soul would never attach to the baby if the mother decided to have an abortion?"

"That is correct."

Inconvenient or permissible?

We start with these two quotes from interviews because both of them have an element that "pro-lifers" will find totally abhorrent. These two entertainers had abortions— several abortions each—because it was too "inconvenient" to have a child. Never mind the fact that at the time when these women were having what Marilyn called her "dalliances," birth control methods were much less certain than they are today. Many pro-lifers will want me to add, no doubt, that sex out of marriage is wrong, and lives such as Marilyn and Carmen lived tend to destroy family life by being sexually promiscuous themselves. Many who hold pro-choice views are just as concerned about family values, though they tend to come at it from another angle.

Before going fully into the background of this issue, we add a third interview we had with the pioneering birth control exponent Margaret Sanger. Unlike Marilyn and Carmen, Margaret managed to have a small family of three children in wedlock, without resorting to abortion. (She did have several sexual partners, however.)

Margaret Sanger

"What's your view of the 'morning-after' pill?"

"Generally, it is a good thing for those who are not ready to experience parenthood when they make the decision to couple, and haven't taken any precautions, and who are in a situation where, because of age, infirmity, and situations such as rape, the woman is not ready to bring another being into the world."

"The next possible stage in the process of ridding oneself of an unwanted child is abortion. What is your attitude toward abortion?"

"At the time of my humanity I considered that if this [pregnancy] was something you had thought out and wanted, it should go forward, regardless of how situations change. But, at the same time, if it were something forced upon you, such as another pregnancy when you already had two or three in diapers, it would be a release. Since now I know that the soul does not enter the body in such circumstances, any of the religious implications of killing a soul—because you cannot kill a soul—are taken out of the mix, and, as with the morning-after pill, I believe that abortion is something which does have its place."

"If I were to argue more sensitively, what about late-term abortions? Isn't there a point where abortion becomes too horrendous to endure?"

"You have to discuss this situation from the spiritual and also the physical viewpoint. The implication upon the body—physically, emotionally, and mentally—is where the person could convince themselves, or society could convince them, that they have killed another human being. That can be devastating. From a spiritual point, again, I know now that you cannot kill the soul, so there would not have been a soul within that agglomeration of cells, regardless of its size, when its growth is terminated."

"Dealing now with women's feelings, some women have had many abortions. Doesn't this harm them spiritually and emotionally?"

"It's their pathway. It gives them spiritual trials, it gives them emotional trials, it gives them mental trials to let them experience and to make choices. This may be the major lesson that they came into this incarnation to learn."

The Masters' teaching

By now we would hope that if you have a point of view about abortion, you have felt it come back up to the surface big time. That's right because the Masters' teaching will take you in another direction altogether. They are in a position to overview all our lives, and the reason why we have come down to live as human beings on planet Earth.

"Please explain the process of incarnation. I understand that a soul, who is a distinct being, comes into relationship with a

body, a physical organism that becomes enlivened by the presence of that soul."
"Correct."

"How is it done?"
"The soul is a spark of light which is a fragment of the Creator. It is an energy able to inhabit many different things. When a soul chooses to experience something it must have the vehicle of a body, a living organism, to do so. It determines, with its council of advisors, what it wishes to experience within the life span of that living vehicle. It then chooses the parentage for that vehicle, who will allow it to be placed into an appropriate situation to experience whatever it has decided to experience.

"So, should the soul want to experience grief, it chooses parents who are going to die, or a family in which there is going to be a physical loss. Therefore it chooses to inhabit the cellular division, the fetus, that occurs from the union of those two parents. The soul generally does not inhabit the growing organism until it is near to birth, but it remains close, monitoring what is going on, to ensure that the circumstances being set up are those which it had anticipated, and which it wants to experience. Sometimes, because of the freedom of choice of the parents, the situation may change; there may be a stillbirth, or some anomaly, so that which is delivered does not need the soul."

"Can a human being exist without a soul?"
"Although a soul may not choose to fully enter a fetus until it is being born, it has to make a connection in order for the fetus to be viable." [*Toni: "They are showing me fine strands between the soul and the fetus."*] "That's how the soul can travel outside the fetus and still maintain the viability of the 'host.' The host in this sense is the body that the soul has chosen to inhabit.

81

"At the moment of conception there is a determination made by each soul that that unique fetus is in fact the chosen one. That's not a connection but an energetic acknowledgment. The soul is aware of the act of conception, but this is not a specific connection. The soul may, in fact, be acting in cooperation with the biological parents to give the urge for the conception at a moment of its choosing. It also determines whether it wants to be male or female."

"How does the soul actually inhabit the physical body: is it by an interface at the cellular level, or at the level of the DNA?"

"It goes into the fetus and brings knowledge of its DNA and its prior experiences—not the DNA strands which have been identified on Earth, but additional strands with which you are unfamiliar. It enters into everything, like a liquid totally saturating a piece of material. It becomes everything that is within the body. In the same way the light—the energy of the soul—comes in contact with the body and can be completely absorbed. In addition to having a connection with that body, the soul can also project out through the ether.

"Then the memories of the soul are downloaded progressively. The soul is still free while the fetus, whose DNA is gradually being filled up, is becoming a storehouse of the knowledge and experience that the soul has had in its prior lives. Ultimately, this part of the physical memory bank is stored in the DNA. Contained within the DNA of the host are all of the soul's memories and lessons, including whatever is desired to be accomplished in this particular incarnation."

"At what point does the total connection take place—if it is, in fact, total?"

"There is no set format. There are instances, with less mature souls in particular, where they enter the fetus almost at the point of conception and remain there. The more experienced souls 'watch the cake baking' but don't become a part of it until it is ready to be 'delivered.' These souls will spend their time elsewhere, saying goodbye to their friends, for example. There is also a small part of the soul left at Home, but the majority of the energy is put into the learning experience.

"For the baby to live apart from the mother, the soul must be inside. The idea is incorrect that the fetus may be delivered and ten minutes later the soul would inhabit it, because within that ten minutes the shell [body] would die. It is rare that the connection between soul and fetus ever takes place after birth. Incorrect readings of this process come from the physical host's faulty memory, not from the facts. It takes a while for the host to be acclimated to the energy of the soul, and to be aware of the point when the two united, which accounts for the occasional incorrect perspective."

Miscarriage and abortion

[*Here we briefly repeat material from the Masters for the sake of completeness.*]
"This topic is a very emotionally charged issue for many human beings. Before we begin let us say clearly that *a soul never dies*. Therefore a miscarriage or an abortion is not the killing or death of a fetal soul. It is the cessation of the bundle of cells that was growing as the result of the union of a sperm and egg.

"Miscarriages are usually the result of a contract made by the mother and father of the cell bundle to deal with all of the emotional results of losing a baby at an early stage of development or even right up to birth [a stillborn baby]. In a very few instances, the soul assigned to a fetus may decide that it is not ready to come to Earth at that time and breaks connection with the fetus, causing it to cease functioning. Remember, the soul always has freedom of choice to do this. "The act of having an abortion is a lesson that some souls wish to experience. All the emotions of selfishness, guilt, regret, disdain, and much more, come flooding in from their self and from their relatives. The woman is in a cauldron of stormy feelings and needs to see the lessons she sought without shutting herself down to the event. When, prior to incarnation, an abortion is arranged as a life event, a soul may not even be assigned to that fetus."

Comment

If you were to ask what is the most significant aspect of the Masters' teaching here, we would repeat without hesitation: "Let us say clearly that a soul never dies." When you think about this, you realize it would be impossible to call souls *eternal souls* if there were any possibility that the soul could be killed. In fact the Masters go further in their teaching: our souls are fragments of Source, the Creator itself. This is a larger issue that deserves a study on its own. Nevertheless their straightforward case is that it is *impossible* to kill the soul.

How then does the soul know how to stay away when an abortion is contemplated? We must not underestimate the workings of the universe. The Masters are quite plain: where an abortion—or a spontaneous miscarriage, or a still-birth—is likely, no soul will be supplied to provide an energetic marker for the fetal tissue. The mother may initially want to bring the baby to term but changes her mind (or is pressured into having an abortion). In this case the soul assigned to the baby withdraws its life support. Souls have no difficulty in hopping out of the fetus. We all do it when we leave our body behind at death. When we die in, say, a vehicle accident or a shooting, we do it so rapidly that our soul has gone before the actual impact that terminates the physical body.

Here is part of another interview, one we had with the film actress Sharon Tate. You may remember that Sharon, married to the film director Roman Polanski, was heavily pregnant with his child when she was stabbed to death by members of the Manson Gang:

Sharon Tate

"You were stabbed 16 times. How much suffering did your soul go through before it left your body?"
    "The perception I had was more of shock and disbelief than actually of any pain in the first several thrusts. After that my soul separated [from my body]."

"Did you have difficulty returning Home?"
    "No, not at all. As soon as I was out of the body and saw everything that was going on, I began to have my memories that I had agreed to be part of this experience on the planet."

"The Masters told us that no soul had been assigned to your unborn baby. Are you aware of this?"
    "Yes."

"Jennifer North, whom you played in Valley of the Dolls, *had an abortion. Did you ever have an abortion?"*
    "Yes."

"Are souls assigned to fetuses that are aborted?"
    "Sometimes. The determining factor is whether the mother, the host of the baby, is to exercise her freedom of choice. Part of her life lesson is to make a decision whether to bring the child into the world, and then, whether to raise the child herself or put the child up for adoption. Since that is freedom of choice, and if it has not already been

determined, in order for that fetus to have a soul if the mother chooses to bear it, a soul has to be assigned."

"So if the mother chose at the last minute to have the child, and walked out of the abortion clinic, would a soul then be assigned to the child if it had not already?"

"A soul would be assigned at the first joining of the sperm and the egg if the fetus is going to have the possibility of going full term."

"And the universe knows whether it will have that possibility because it sees into the future?"

"The universe is aware of the mother's desired life lesson. Unless the mother has chosen from the very beginning to have an abortion, so that she has to deal for the rest of her incarnation with all the guilt and the energy surrounding her thinking that she has killed another individual, a soul will have been assigned."

"In the case of your abortion, was the soul assigned?"
"No."

"Do souls directly involved in an abortion procedure suffer?"

"No, they never suffer, because the soul is just loosely connected with the fetus until it comes out. The only time that a soul may experience something is in the case of a baby going through difficulty at the time of delivery, such as a breech birth with the cord around its neck, or something like that. Then a soul may experience something. But that's a lesson that's been set up ahead of time, to go through the struggle, whether it has the strength to hold on and to make it through the difficulty, and whether it wants to come out as an injured human from some birth problem, to deal with that throughout the rest of its incarnation."

Mother Teresa

Some of the interviews we conducted involved leading figures from the Christian, Jewish, and Hindu communities. The viewpoint of these leaders concerning their religion's teaching about faith and morals was often modified or had even been starkly changed since their return Home. Issues that they embraced are turned on their heads, and strongly held points of view are abandoned.

Few people are more revered than Mother Teresa:

"I see all issues concerning human bodies as involving contracts, which are not just between a single body and one other individual but between a group of souls who are going to share some aspect of that body's existence.

"When it comes to abortion, the contracts may not even involve a soul. A soul may not be assigned or may not have chosen that particular conglomerate of cells, knowing that it is not going to go through the entire gestational process. Again, it comes down to lessons that have to be learned by the various parties: mother, father, extended family members, sometimes society in general. It is what needs to be experienced and therefore is neither right nor wrong. You cannot kill a soul—it is impossible to kill a soul. That soul has agreed to the situation—if there is even a soul involved—surrounding that abortion."

Pope John XXIII

The reforming Pope, John XXIII, is more controversial. His statement is also the most stark comment we have received:

"Does the church's strong emphasis on social issues, such as abortion and divorce, represent a balanced view of the social teaching of Jesus?"

"No. The teachings of Jesus were that people would feel their connection with their soul on the planet, to experience things to bring them more into love, the unconditional love of God the Creator. There are certain things that must be experienced for that to occur.

"My feeling on abortion (and I believed it up until my transition) was that the soul enters the cells that become the fetus, at the time of conception. I now know that is not true. The soul chooses its time of entry, and sometimes goes in and out of the fetus before it becomes a viable human. I have also had my memory refreshed, that sometimes an abortion is a lesson that must be borne by the woman so that she may learn some of the various issues which she came down to the planet to learn. Abortion is not the killing of a soul, because the soul can never be killed. The soul never dies; it goes on, and it may not even be in that bundle of cells that is growing, and it won't be there at the time of an abortion."

"Don't those who proclaim the sanctity of life have a valid point about cruelty to the unborn, and about the casual way abortion is sometimes treated? Isn't the idea of the sanctity of life—in the light of abortion and of life-support issues—of merit?"
"The cruelty you mention would be cruelty only if the soul were in the body. If a person has a growth within their body, a cancerous tumor, is it cruel to remove that tumor? That tumor has no soul; it has no connection to the spiritual, except while it is in the body when there is a stream of consciousness of the energy of the soul within it. But at the time of its removal it does not contain a soul. The same thing is true of a fetus; it does not contain a soul at the time of the abortion or the removal, so, therefore, it cannot be an issue of cruelty."

On the issue of abortion the Pope really appeared to pull the rug out from under the Roman Catholic church's current teaching. The soul of a child does not actually enter the embryonic cells at conception, and anyway, it would not be trapped or killed by an abortion. So removal of a fetus is no more grave a procedure than removal of a cancerous growth. Abortion may well exist to teach both parents and society a lesson, but there is no cruelty to the unborn involved in the procedure.

Learning our lessons

The Masters teach that we have identified those types of experience we need, during our time on Earth, for personal growth. We select our parents, and our soul makes contracts with other souls to provide challenges of various kinds during our lifetime. Our physical experiences are always for a positive purpose within the life of our soul. As in the abortion situation, lessons will not necessarily be pleasant or even positive (such as a girl, pressured to have an abortion, feels it is wrong). This may involve us in role-plays that human ethics may consider profoundly evil. These experiences help us to gain a better understanding of the opposite of negativity—our soul's own unconditional love.

Our soul never dies because it remains always pure energy in harmony with the eternal Source. This fact affects many areas of human life and death. For example, abortion is seen by souls at Home as a non-issue. The aborted soul (if a soul was ever assigned to the fetus) is not involved in the destruction of fetal tissue and it returns Home well in advance of the procedure. That being so, it is the emotional experience of the abortion by mother, father, family friends and society that is the real lesson to be learned.

The ego and the soul

The Masters: "The polarity of planet Earth creates a unique thing within the human body which is called the ego and is the Earth-master. It tells people whether they are rich, successful, popular, or playing the game of life as their society wants it played.

"The measurement device of the ego is judgment. This calculates right or wrong according to the recognized belief systems of others. Ego takes all decisions out of people's hands and places them in the hands of the society. Everything people do gets judged. Consequently, individuals never ask themselves whether they feel like doing something, but rather want to know what is expected of them."

When dealing with abortion we find ourselves in the middle of a human situation shot through with the ego-judgment of society. It is a battleground! Everybody is more than willing to gave us their opinion and sign us up as a true believer on one side or another. So our soul must become aware of its own power. It must recognize its ability to make choices and then to evaluate everything it sees for itself. It must also decide if something can be learned from a situation, like an abortion, and whether or not it is something that needs to be repeated in that lifetime.

"Facts with which the ego deals come from outside the body. They are put into the brain through the eyes or the ears. Knowledge with which the soul deals can be found within. It comes from comparing feelings about its experiences with feelings of unconditional love."

Summary

The view from the Other Side is an appraisal made with a clear understanding of what goes on in human life. In regard to the issue of abortion, the Masters' viewpoint makes possible the following points:

(1) The soul is eternal, part of the creative energy of Source. You cannot kill the soul. This is a real challenge to those who insist that abortion "murders" children. If you are prepared to see, as the Masters do, that for a fetus to become a child it must have its spiritual connection intact through the indwelling of a soul, then, since the soul is indestructible and leaves the fetus before the procedure, the destruction of a fetus cannot be the murder of a child.

(2) The majority of abortions have been set up in advance of the mother's incarnating, as a learning exercise by the mother's soul (with or without the father and other members of the family and circle of friends). This decision, to experience such trauma, is part of a larger plan by which souls come to planet Earth to experience negativity, either by suffering or by perpetrating negative behavior. The decision is so clear in many cases that the universal forces do not even arrange for a soul to be present during gestation.

(3) Society tells us what to think about such matters as abortion. The view of society does not always fit in with the spiritual need of mothers who have become pregnant in circumstances that are abhorrent or unworkable. Since abortion, as seen by the spirit world, does not represent murder, the needs of the mother are rightly to be evaluated by her soul, and the social and psychological consequences of her decision to abort represent a lesson, first to her, and

then to the wider society as a whole. What the lesson is, precisely, depends on where the mother and those who surround her are at the time, and the reaction of the wider community—including the prevailing judgment of religious leaders.

~ * ~

Health and Healing

The Masters wrote this essay

One of the ways every soul uses to learn lessons when incarnate on Earth is through different things occurring in the human body. These are felt in the physical existence by variances in the health or balance of the body. The lesson is to understand the dis-ease [lack of balance], deal with the implications of the unbalance, and find out enough about yourself to influence the effects. Health issues impact the mental, emotional, and spiritual growth of each incarnation. We are seeking to give you a little idea of how these things fit together. We do not consider health to refer only to the functioning of the human body but to anything that affects its perfection.

Contracts use negative energy. You incarnate to learn. You decide what you are going to experience, either within certain categories (e.g., mental stress, physical complaints, emotional instability), or by certain specific problems you desire to explore. In most cases you will need others' interaction to get the full impact of your choice, so you make contracts with people to be there to provide that interaction.

Learn the essence of the soul

When we speak of the life journey of a soul as a study in bringing an awareness of the essence of our being into the

93

arena of physical living, we mean reaching an understanding of everything we have planned, done (both successfully and unsuccessfully), and seen during an incarnation. We first evaluate those things by the emotional impact on our physical selves. We later see if we have gained enough knowledge on the subject to add to our overall wisdom. Let us see a few examples of these simple lessons.

Self-worth is a valuable lesson that each soul works into its life. If you cannot find a sense of your own importance, and the power of your essence as a piece of the Source, you will not be able to clearly see the other lessons you are working through. Others help you with this lesson by throwing you into judging your actions against what others have seemingly achieved. A healthy self-worth evaluates only if you are learning something about living.

Self-confidence is important to you to allow you to stick up for yourself and to work your way through the belief systems society has established so you may learn how to exercise the freedom of choice that puts you in control of your challenges. You will be constantly confronted by the world with suggestions they feel are essential to your life. Your job is to feel what is the healthy and necessary path for your growth.

Assuming responsibility is a necessary step in the directing of your learning process. If you continue to depend on others to tell you what to do you never exercise your freedom of choice and therefore can't gain wisdom. Think of a seed that should prosper but is afraid to break out of the ground to be nourished by the sun. It is comfortable in the warmth of the earth but it cannot grow. The seed has to break out of its comfort zone, stand on its own, and decide where and how to grow. A healthy life is one filled with growth based on your own decision of choices because you want to have the final say.

Graceful dependency is another aspect of the philosophy of living. It does not contradict assuming responsibility, but rather allows you to truly depend on others to help set up your life lessons. Respect the contracts that you have made, and do not "blame" another person for placing you into a situation that is needed for learning if it is a negative lesson. You set up the situation, so work through it instead of spending all your time and effort getting revenge for a perceived wrong. The universe is helping you.

Going with the flow is being present in the moment at all times. This is a way of being in a healthy balance with all the energy in the universe. You are not reliving the past nor spending your conscious time minutely planning the future. You just are! The universe will bring to you what you desire to experience, but you can't "see" it if you are not in balance the moment it appears. So sit back and allow yourself to be present.

Creativity is part of your energy. All souls have the ability to manifest that which they need to complete their mission on Earth. As a fragment of Source you have the power inside to produce the situations you are ready to experience. You must accept that you have the ability before you can use it. Going into your heart and feeling the energy in your life will tell you first what you need, second what you need to create for a successful lesson, and finally exactly how to manifest all the parts.

Experience judgment

While the soul is in a society of humans, who are necessary to set up life lessons, the only way to determine success and progress is with judgment. The Earth is a duality and the ego judges what is healthy and in balance, or unhealthy and out of balance. If everyone on the planet had a medical condition—say, cancer—then being debilitated by cancer would be a normal, or healthy, stage in life. You see such medical conditions as abnormal and unhealthy because most of society does not suffer from them at the same time. They are considered to be bad, harmful, and wrong, regardless of the fact that they are a spiritual teaching tool.

Sometimes your lesson is to battle a medical condition. When this occurs it is your job to find out why you have the condition, what it means to you and those around you, and if ridding yourself of it is expected. To the conscious human mind an illness or dis-ease is something to be rid of at all costs. Forget that the occurrence may give you awareness of your spiritual path for the first time. It may bring the people you have contracts with to your vicinity. But you will miss all of this if you are only concerned with "beating" the medical condition.

Understand who is in charge in your life. You have ultimate control unless you give your power to someone else to make decisions for you. If you have chosen to go through this life needing the assistance of others for daily maintenance, it may seem as if they are in control. They are in control of the physical aspects of life, but you remain totally in control over what you learn from this experience.

In that situation there are two kinds of health: the physical health of the body (your shell), and the health of your soul as seen through your mental and emotional condition. If you take part in decisions concerning your care, you are working on the lessons that you set up to learn. If you do nothing but fight the energies—living in a state of sadness, anger, and victimization—you will not understand why you chose this life. Always ask, "How do I feel about my situation?" That will tell you what you came to work on.

Comfort and Choice

Finding and grasping your comfort level is a means of understanding your reason for being on Earth. What we mean by "comfort level" is your accepting the state of your body.

If your body is missing a part or two, or refuses to be perfect by the standards of society, how do you feel about your life? Do you make the most of the lessons it brings your way? Or do you feel miserable and share that misery with anyone who comes close to you?

Your health is out of balance if you cannot find the love of self telling you that this is exactly where you planned to be at this time. When you love yourself, exactly as you are, it is possible to start working on the lessons that resulted in your body's not meeting the perfect norm. Knowing who you are, a magnificent piece of Source, your soul will always feel it resides in a comfort level from which it may venture into negativity to get an idea of its lessons and be able to work on them.

Learn how to take back your power. When people feel overwhelmed by their situation they sit back and tell the world, "Go ahead and do whatever you want to do to me!" This is giving away all your power—to decide, learn, and thrive—to whoever wants to grab it. You will be unable to fulfill your desires for knowledge and wisdom, because you are just like a powerless boat on the ocean being battered by the wind and waves. To affect your course in life you have to be controlling the rudder of your boat as it moves forward. You have to acknowledge what is happening and decide to take action. Then you are truly empowered.

Exercising freedom of choice is one of the most important aspects of the incarnation experience. Everything that a soul does in its entire existence (which is endless) is directed by its own freedom of choice. No other being can affect you in any way, shape, or form, unless you allow it. If a person says something that, based on society's judgmental standard, would be hurtful to you, it will only feel hurtful if you let it. Before you can feel hurt, you have to believe there is truth in what is being said, and accept that somehow it is your fault.

No part of your life is written in stone. You had made some decisions about what you wanted to experience once you got to Earth, but you never specified all the particulars. This is where your freedom of choice comes in. How do you want to experience that betrayal? What about abandonment or abuse? You pick the scenarios. And once a scene begins, you choose who becomes involved and when to change direction or call a halt. Part of the human decision-making process involves deciding how the body is going to be treated. Being aware of the diseases and conditions that can affect the body, some souls spend a portion of their time on strengthening and preparing the body to prevent the majority of ailments.

All the energy in the universe is accessible to every soul. It is used through the practice of unconditional love. This energy is perfect in every way. It has the ability to bring all physical things into balance, that is, into a healed state— a state of self-love and acceptance.

Means of healing

We will now discuss various means of healing, before and after awareness takes place:

Preventive measures are choices such as physical practices, lifestyles, and the use of natural substances that help you prevent ill health. It must be noted here that regardless what you do in your physical life to prevent a condition, if before incarnating you had made plans for that experience, you will not be able to prevent its occurrence. You will be able to affect its severity and whether or not you can rid your body of the effects—unless it was pre-determined to be a fatal condition.

Exercise physically strengthens the body and causes the internal systems to work efficiently. A strenuous regime takes a lot of discipline (which also may be part of the life lessons) and facilitates healing because the body is used to working to bring health to all its parts. Therefore, a broken bone heals more easily, and a condition that makes you bedridden for a period of time is easier to recuperate from because your body yearns for activity.

Energy practices such as Tai Chi, Qigong, Yoga, and Meditation are all preventive in that they impart a sense of what is happening in the body, so that at the first sign of illness, the person is aware of it and can start the healing process. These practices involve consciousness of the universal life force energy's entering the body and of the chi (self-energy flow) within the body.

Energy practices—Reiki, Pranic Healing, Therapeutic Touch, Quantum Touch, and many more modalities—generally involve the help of a second person to ensure that the healthy flow of your chi is assisted by the life force energy, boosted by the practitioner. All energy work has an influence on the mental and emotional condition of the person, as well as the physical. The flow of the energy will dislodge blockages and impact your mood for a period of time, so it also has a clearing effect. These modalities are used to get people in touch with themselves.

Tai Chi is a series of exercises that assist balance (so you don't fall) and flexibility (so you don't strain or tear something), putting you into an awareness of your body's condition. It is very slow-moving exercise, perfect for all ages and conditions. If practiced frequently, it produces calmness and peacefulness without stress.

Qigong is an offshoot of martial arts practices that connects practitioners to their mental and spiritual selves. It also provides all the benefits of Tai Chi. The purpose is seeking total body awareness, which is important in the busy world where it is common to ignore little pains and distractions until they are huge enough to sideline you from your daily work.

Yoga seeks to provide the body with perfect spiritual insight and tranquility through forming postures, during which meditation is employed. There are many types of yoga, and some near-religious practices may be involved. Here, we consider it a good way to prevent dis-ease from creeping up on you, and a means of increasing energy flow to cleanse dis-ease from the body.

Meditation is a word that means hundreds of different things in your world. We use it here to refer to the state of perfect communication between your conscious mind and your unconscious awareness, and also communication with the non-physical beings who are around to assist you with your difficulties. Meditation involves clearing your mind of all conscious thoughts, and then existing in that quietude to access information about your body, your emotions, and your mental state. It can be your early warning system to spotlight matters in your life that need attention.

Homeopathic Medicine uses the principle of "like cures like." A highly diluted amount of a poison is introduced into the body to prevent the corresponding illness or negative reaction. The body becomes sensitized to invasion and builds up a defensive resistance. This same principle is employed with vaccinations, but homeopathic substances are more highly diluted than vaccines. The same substances may be used to treat a patient who has contracted the illness—which cannot be said for vaccines.

Herbal Medicines were the forerunners of modern-day medicine. From the beginning of human history it was recognized that certain parts of plants, seeds, roots, bark, and leaves—when taken as is or made into a tea, poultice, or extraction—cured, healed, or at least soothed the sick patient.

Modern pharmacology grew out of humans' taking these substances, first by using them in their natural state, and then by chemically reproducing them so people didn't have to go out into the wild to get more. A resurgence is occurring wherein you are understanding that the chemical mixtures (modern day prescriptions) have a lot of harmful and unnecessary substances within them. Pure herbal preparations contain no preservatives, additives, or artificial coloring—and fewer side effects.

Herbal essences are now available on a commercial basis. Makers prepare tinctures in dropper bottles so you may carry a medicine cabinet with you. A couple of drops under the tongue—where the mixture can immediately enter the bloodstream—calms, corrects, or cures the threatened ailment. These are pure substances without additives, and are easy to transport. It is very much like early man who, suffering from stomach cramps, grabbed a leaf off a known plant and, after chewing on it for a short time, was able to go on his way pain free. Flower essences, too, can be effective in altering energy and promoting healing.

Crystals carry vibrational energy that may be felt, consciously or unconsciously, on the body or nervous system. Healing and balancing crystal energies are used to modify a negative energy that is affecting the physical body by resonating with it at the level of the body's human frequencies and bringing them into balance.

There is not only a single energy involved, but vibrations in the area of sound, color, and light waves. Each of these has its own impact on the body. Crystals naturally boost and amplify the body's own rhythms, bringing them into resonance with the flow of universal energy, which is always in perfect balance and therefore heals the physical. Crystals can also deter negative or harmful energy from affecting the body.

Ayurveda, a holistic science of health and healing practices, originated in India over 5,000 years ago. The name comes from two Sanskrit words: *Ayu* meaning life, and *Veda*, which means knowledge or science. It therefore may be said to be the science of life. The practices may be used only for healing, but most practitioners have adopted various exercises as a way for living. The philosophy of Ayurveda treats the whole person—body, mind, and spirit—as a means of prevention, so that treatment of an ailment is not necessary because the body remains dis-ease free.

Substances employed in Ayurveda are primarily herb based. A variety of diets help strengthen against and treat adverse conditions, while breathing and physical exercises, massage, cleansing, and meditation prepare the body and its spiritual, non-physical side to come into alignment with the universe.

Treatments

The form of treatment for bodily ailments you will think about to ease your medical condition depends on where you live in the world, your background, and your philosophy of life. In Western society, and a lot of Eastern Europe, allopathic (non-homeopathic)—also called "modern"—medicine is the popular choice. In Asia, there is some allopathic medicine but also holistic, homeopathic remedies, and Ayurveda. In indigenous areas, the shaman, medicine man, or *curandero* provides care.

A second layer of treatment uses non-traditional methods that address the spiritual, mental, and emotional aspects of the person. This generally occurs by approaching the unconscious mind in a variety of ways to release—in order to deal with them—hidden things that are manifesting physical symptoms. The methods range from medicinal psychiatry to hypnosis, along with intention-driven practices such as energy work, prayer, EFT, visualization, and self-healing.

Allopathic modern Western medical practitioners are generally designated by the MD (Medical Doctor) letters following their names. These people go through rigorous training in the treatment of symptoms. Yes, we said "symptoms," not patients. The basis of the practice is to recognize a pattern of activity (listed in the medical books), such as a high blood pressure reading or the sound of an irregular heart rhythm, and then treat the problem with a prescription of medicine. A broken bone has prescribed patterned treatment, as do diseased organs that must be removed from the body cavity.

During all of its history, conventional medicine has overlooked patients' attitudes about their condition. The latest wrinkle by MDs is to investigate the involvement of their patients' intention in healing. Reiki and other energy modalities, as well as meditation, prayer, and visualization, are now being tested for their input and influence on the healing process. For the first time, doctors are starting to acknowledge that they may not be the only factor at work in the healing process.

Psychiatry, Counseling, and Hypnotherapy are methods of working with the mind and the unconscious as means of allowing the body to aid in its own healing. Each of these processes engages the thinking mind to look deeper into the unconscious to find the causes of health problems. While the majority of such problems will be mental and emotional, a physical condition may also result when the unconscious either convinces people that they need to deal with some issue, or blocks them from seeing a connection between their current dis-ease and a past event.

Psychiatry is a medical specialty where the doctor uses conversation and penetrating thought to delve into the patient's subconscious, together with providing prescription drugs to alter patients' thinking or moods through interference with their brain waves. Very few psychiatrists view their work as having spiritual implications. Their field is seen as having to do with the problems they treat. Their patients merely show up with mental aberrations rather than physical ones, such as broken bones.

A lot of the treatments employed in psychiatry use coping skills. These are procedures that teach, or allow, patients to change their behavior patterns, so that the underlying cause of their condition is hidden deeper and doesn't have as much of an impact on their life. The problem with this is that the cause is never really addressed. While the patients may appear to get better, the cause of their problem is hidden behind more walls and may reemerge.

Remember, everything occurring in your human incarnation is some piece of a life lesson experienced for you to gain the knowledge and wisdom behind the exercise. It won't go away until you understand it.

Counseling (sometimes recently called life coaching) is employed by practitioners who, in various ways, can help individuals to understand and work through the confusion in which they find themselves. The majority of counselors specialize in an area such as abuse, addiction, anxiety, co-dependency, grief, or personal-image issues. As with psychiatrists, most also use coping skills to divert the thought process of the client. There is a growing number of counselors who recognize that the person is experiencing a spiritual situation and needs help in seeing it clearly as a life lesson, or an issue from another life. They will then work with the client to bring a degree of understanding into that person's life so he or she may carry on.

Hypnotherapy is the practice of assisting a person into a state of relaxation, moving away from the conscious thought processes to enable access to the unconscious mind. The unconscious mind is the gateway to the soul, and to knowledge of everything the soul has planned for that lifetime and what it has done in past lifetimes. Barriers and restrictive belief systems are all moved aside, and the soul, sometimes called the "higher self," may come and assist in completing the task in which a client is stuck. A difficulty may be encountered if the therapist fails to see the revelations that come out in the sessions as indications of a soul's journey, but thinks that they are fabrications that merely need to be adjusted by post-hypnotic suggestions to balance up the client's psyche.

Spiritual hypnotherapists will deal with the higher self as a guide to the issues that must be addressed first. They will also communicate with the soul to see if there are any negative attachments it has gathered in an attempt to learn something about the human experience. In this type of therapy, the client will be directed to look into the soul's records to see whether a current problem originates from another lifetime, and the individual still carries the energy of an uncompleted lesson.

Energy clearing and balancing, acupuncture, and chakra balancing are methods of energetically working to remove blockages resulting from the way people have lived their life. The body has become sluggish and gathered refuse. Each of these procedures works with major pathways of energy as they travel through the body. By external stimulation, energy is brought back into balance after clearing out anything restricting its flow. The body, in working through its lessons, has a certain amount of debris that has collected, like byproducts of nutrition. Just like the body's need to eliminate waste, it also needs to balance up its energy by eliminating excesses and residual rubbish.

Prayer, EFT, visualization, affirmations are a few of the practices that bridge the conscious and unconscious mind to assist in balancing the body back to health. They all deal with procedures people become mindfully involved in, with the intent that they will change the future.

Prayer is a procedure that a majority of people grew up believing in as the only non-physical source of assistance when they or others were in poor health. It is primarily based on the fact that many religions hold there is a supreme being who has total control and judgment over everything that happens to humanity. Prayer is taught as the proper way to entreat this being to look favorably upon the poor human and to restore health. It suggests that patients themselves have no say in returning to balance.

Since all souls are broken off from Source, the point of origin of everything that exists, each of you has the power to do what you used to believe could only be done by the supreme being, generally referred to as "God." If you pray that you will understand what is causing your condition, and pray that you will have the strength to tap into your essence so you may correct all difficulties, your prayer will be answered. And did you notice the prayer was to yourself?

EFT (Emotional Freedom Technique) combines a mental procedure with a physical tapping on the skin at various acupuncture and acupressure points that overlay the body's energy meridians. Conscious thoughts are directed toward the behavior or problem that is being addressed. The client repeats a phrase patterned like: "Even though I have a fear of water (or whatever the problem is), I forgive myself and I love myself unconditionally." This is accompanied by tapping over the energy centers that unconsciously reinforce the positive self-love statement. If the client believes the issue can be released, it will depart, and any additional tapping keeps it from recurring.

A potential problem with this technique is when the cause is not really known and therefore is incapable of being addressed. What then happens is that a coping skill covers up the underlying cause until it finds another more powerful way to surface.

Visualization is seeing in your mind the result you desire— a dis-ease-free body. If you truly believe you have the power to create what you are seeing, and all doubts are kept at bay, you become what you see. In difficult cases, such as broken bones, the client may see a miniature construction crew working on healing the bone by sealing it with some type of liquefied bone fragments. If the break was bad, the crew may need to place a support within before sealing it up.

This may be done as a supplement to allopathic medicine. The doctor may set the bone, possibly inserting a pin, and then encase it in a plaster cast. Consider that your healing is being done on the spiritual level, via the ether, to assist and speed up the physical process.

Affirmation can be one of the first steps people may take in changing the way they feel about a health problem. It is common, particularly when mental or emotional conditions are causing health problems, to be dealing with a total sense of helplessness. "I can't do anything, it is too difficult." That simple feeling and statement tells your body it is all right for you to continue having the problem—that you believe you need it to carry on with your life.

To allow any kind of treatment—either physical or non-physical—to impact your dis-ease, you must have the mental belief that you deserve to be healed. If you make and continue to repeat a statement like, "I am in perfect health," that tells your unconscious that you have to assist in getting rid of anything unhealthy. You won't believe it at first, but if you keep saying it long enough, it will start to sound possible, then probable, and then your natural state of existence. This is the old "fake it until you make it" practice.

Self-healing is the last important type of healing. As we have mentioned in a number of the treatments, the patient's attitude is as important as, if not more so than, the curative techniques that are employed. All healing aspects have two important factors: practitioners, whether doctors or therapists, and (most importantly) the patients themselves. If injured, sick, or deranged people do not think they can be healed, cured, or balanced, they never will be.

All dis-eases are part of your life lessons. The soul's purpose is to discover its own powerful essence, allowing it to make choices of life experiences, and if it never accepts its ability to be whole, it never will.

Discovery of the cause

Finding a cause becomes important when you know an ailment is part of a life lesson, but you have no idea of the nature of that lesson. You may never be able to get back to perfect health if you don't discover the cause. Here are a number of ways to work on finding the tasks hidden behind the Earthly difficulties:

Following your own doubts and fears takes you on the easiest path into your life lessons. Your lessons are set up to force you to make decisions—to use your freedom of choice. One way you can tell when such a situation is in front of you is by fearing the next step or doubting that what you have always done is not the thing that is the best way for you to learn.

When we say following your doubting and fearful energies, we mean going into the reason they have popped up in the first place. You find yourself in fear and you freeze, not wanting to do something wrong or have something hurtful happen to you, and you are totally paralyzed by your own thought process. You can banish the problem by finding the cause of the fear. It's in your subconscious. How do you access it? You dive into your inner self, to the feelings that are in the background when the fear is at center stage.

The process goes like this: The question you put to yourself is, "What am I feeling right now?" Recognize the feeling (e.g., never being able to succeed). Then the next thing you ask is, "Where did that feeling originate?" Your intuition will hear that it came from parent, teacher, or someone else. So the next question you ask is, "Do I really believe that is true at this time?" If the answer is "no," you may erase it from your psyche and proceed. If the answer is "yes" or "maybe," then you recount all the times in this life when you have been fabulously successful. You then can rewrite that fear with the knowledge that you can succeed at whatever you engage your full mind and being in attempting.

Hypnosis includes past-life regression (PLR), and life-between-lives regression (LBL). These involve techniques wherein a hypnotherapist may help you to find what blockages are stopping your healing progress. These are particularly necessary when you are not able to do this work by yourself. Sometimes your conscious mind is so active or strong it will not allow you to delve into your unconscious alone. Then these practices will assist.

The visualization process directed by a trained hypnotherapist can help you to find things that have been hiding from your conscious awareness, and have been unconsciously patterning your behavior. The technique is merely one of relaxing your conscious mind so that it takes a vacation, or becomes dormant, while the practitioner talks with your unconscious or higher mind.

This aspect of you has a record of everything that has ever happened to you, both in the present incarnation and any other time your soul has chosen to have duality experiences. By inquiring why a problem is holding you back, your higher mind will let you see, or remember, what life lesson you did not complete; or an energy, such as revenge, that you chose to carry over until you were ready to deal with it. Once the problem is acknowledged or brought into your awareness, you may finish up the task and not have it bother you any longer.

Past-life regression is a powerful hypnotic process that brings forward uncompleted prior lessons that you chose to keep around until you learned everything about them. The hypnotist has you visualize yourself into a state away from your conscious mind, and then asks you when you first experienced the particular difficulty you are having in your current life. This will take you back into a former life where the same energy gave you problems.

Say, you are unable to have any confidence in your decisions. You then find in a past life you were a military commander. You lost all your troops because you think you made the wrong tactical decision, and you swore never to trust yourself again—and you haven't been able to, even in this subsequent life. In the PLR you find that the reason everyone was killed was not caused by your decision but by the fact that you had a traitor in your midst who sold you out to the enemy. This will allow you to forgive yourself for something you didn't do anyway, and start to trust yourself again. Problem solved.

Life-between-lives (LBL) regression is the ability to enter into the space between incarnations when you are at Home. This allows access to the reasons you have planned certain things for this lifetime, a list of the unfinished business you are carrying over, and the wisdom you have accumulated in past lives. This also allows you to rejuvenate within the unconditional love of the universe, and remember the whole person for the human life experience.

This LBL state brings you closest to understanding the spiritual aspects of your journey. It is a fantastic step along the road to total awareness of the process of reincarnation. It can only accomplish that task, however, when you have dealt with all the human life lessons still unresolved.

Meditation has many purposes for human beings. It may be used to reduce stress, balance energies such as heart rate and blood pressure, go inside to your higher self, and communicate with non-physical beings. The only way it aids in discovering the cause of your problems is when it is used for communication and not body manipulation.

The state of meditation is one in which your conscious thinking mind is disconnected from awareness. The thinking mind is the product of the ego, which functions by judging every action performed (or thought about) by the body. In order to judge anything, you need to be constantly comparing your thoughts against whatever society thinks is the correct way to do things. This removes decisions from you and gives them to "people" out there. You will never learn anything about your intention for own journey by being connected to the matrix of the living.

Meditation as a spiritual tool involves a total disconnect from the human world and a plug-in to the non-physical universe. In the quiet of unconditional universal love you may access all your guides, your records, and your friends. You may get the answers to your questions and suggestions from others whose only purpose is helping you complete your incarnation.

Modern Western techniques include physical ways that can be used to help discover the causes of illness and disease. These include simple mechanical tests to find mental, psychological, and physical causes. The problem is that their findings are then interpreted by humans using human standards and establishing a norm. They do not see the interplay of past lives, the soul planning, or completion of contracts set up to assist you and others with your desires. But, on the other hand, the interpretation of these tests sometimes provides for you to use your freedom of choice for the next step in your journey.

Faith in yourself

Without an understanding of your personal growth, and an attempt to find out who and what you are, you will not have any awareness of the spiritual mission you have chosen for yourself. As a human characteristic, your basic need is to have faith in yourself, to develop a set of rules (called a belief system), and, by using whatever it takes, to have the feeling you are doing what you came to Earth to do.

Creating a belief system is accomplished by using your freedom of choice to decide what you want to do in each phase of your life. The problem with this seemingly simple task is that society makes it difficult for you to prefer your choices to theirs. From the very beginning of life the human child is indoctrinated with being part of the crowd. You should always do as you are told. You must follow the rules that your family or society thinks are best. At this point in your life you are unaware you have any choices.

As adulthood dawns you are a picture of your upbringing, acting, like any "good little soldier," by the rules and regulations with which you were raised. This is true, even if the exact nature of those rules is unknown to you. Society says that's the way things have always been done and must be done. This is when your feelings help you to find out that you truly do have choices. You begin to see that certain actions do not resonate or feel good to you. Your choice then is to follow the pack or take off in another direction. You make your own decisions.

When you start to diverge from your inbred beliefs, you will create your own belief system. You will find that, as you progress, your beliefs will change with your increase in knowledge and understanding. You are finding out who you are as a soul, and that you are using the lessons you came to learn as guideposts. You are finally really living!

Five steps to becoming who you choose to be

You will never feel that you are balanced, or in excellent health, unless you are leading the life you choose to lead. So how do you get there? By five steps, but notice we did not say "easy" steps. This is the core of the process of enlightenment, the theme of the wheel of rebirth, putting the whole together in a peak experience. We think you will have an idea of their importance.

Step One: Accept your true nature as a piece of the creative Source. Simply put, you know all, can do all, can experience anything you desire, and can be anything you choose. You need to accept your soul as your identity and your power as your driving force.

Step Two: Have faith in yourself, and realize the importance of self-confidence and self-worth—if you don't feel the flow of energy in the life around you, you cannot change it. Have faith in whatever your inner voice tells you is the direction you need. Get out of your head—the source of society's thinking—and get into your heart instead.

Step Three: Believe your nature is within you at all times, even in the frail human body that now encloses your soul. Believe with your whole being that you have the ability to access your nature at any time you desire. Believe that you are in charge of your soul's learning experience.

Step Four: Know, and then take a leap of faith so that you can bring all your abilities into action. Right about now we are hearing the question: "Wait, if I believe already, what is this knowing business? Aren't they the same?" No way! You can believe you have the ability to run a marathon, but until you prepare for one you don't really know that you can complete it. Knowing is necessary for the final step.

Step Five: Become what you accept you are. You are an immortal soul. Have faith in your abilities as a piece of Source, believing you can use your abilities to be in perfect balance and health in this incarnation. Knowing you can do this, you begin the process. Then, low and behold, you have become that which you sought!

Affirmation

We have already discussed this powerful tool. It is no more than combining simple words in life-altering statements. Using that same technique, you may accomplish the five steps, changing your conscious thinking about each step. And as we said before, if you say it, if you hear it, you can accept it as true. It is a mindset change.

"Fake it till you make it." To some people this may seem like cheating. The truth of the matter is anytime people change jobs or start a new career, they fake it until they make themselves believe that they can tackle the required new procedures. Someone fresh out of medical school isn't an experienced doctor; someone new to ice skates isn't an accomplished figure skater; and a brand new parent certainly isn't a fantastic caregiver. But by faking it, keeping working at it, and believing in themselves, eventually they become experts. So can you.

Important Note

The information contained in this chapter is intended to be educational information only and not for the diagnosis, prescription, or treatment of any medical or psychological condition. If you need medical advice you should contact a licensed healthcare professional. The authors and publishers are in no way liable for the misuse of this material.

Exploring Reincarnation

Heaven, Hell, and Suicide

The simple answer

Are there such places as heaven and hell? We have all been given the idea that there are.

Most people in the Western world take it for granted that heaven is a place where there is a reward given for people living a good life, and hell is a place of punishment for wicked people. Our culture is built on the reward or punishment idea. Associated with this is the idea of God, the divine judge who knows our lives intimately and judges us on our track record. But we do not understand the basis for such reward and punishment. Some people look to God as kind, generous, forgiving; others perceive God as stern, exacting, wrathful, and avenging. Some think that their good works lead to rewards and heaven; others say that we are saved from hell by the gift of faith in Jesus Christ.

"Not so fast," say the Masters. "You've got it all wrong."

Yes, heaven truly is a benign feeling we have during our lifetime; we can also make or suffer a hell in our mind. But neither heaven nor hell exists for us when we go Home to the Other Side. Home is a place of unconditional love and is entirely free from judgment. All souls eventually go Home. There is neither a heaven nor a hell to go to, and no divine judge to send us there.

117

More from the Masters:

"Home is a place of continuous unconditional love. Duality exists only on planet Earth. The concept of heaven and hell is of polar opposites and exists only on Earth. Many religious organizations use the idea of heaven and hell as a reward or a punishment for following or not following their beliefs, rules, and regulations. This is an invention of the ego, which wants to make judgments on all activities. It is a means of controlling people who are told, 'Do as we say or suffer the consequences.'

"Heaven exists on Earth in the form of happiness, familial love, and sharing and caring between people. Hell exists on Earth in the form of oppression, murder, and abuse. A soul can also create a hell it may feel it deserves, such as cancer. Once the soul leaves the body it enters a state of unconditional love, void of any judgment concerning its actions on Earth connected with the lessons it decided to experience in that life. There is nothing to be condemned or rewarded."

George S. Patton

We continue with quotes from the souls of famous people who have spoken to us. First, US General George S. Patton of World War II fame. This was a tough soldier who hated any action by his soldiers that he considered cowardice, and punished them severely for it:

"There is no hell except what you create for yourself on Earth. The battlefield was hell. Moving into places we had to destroy, in order to be victorious in our pursuits, created a hell. Hell is a physical thing. It is not an energetic, spiritual thing. In spirit form there is nothing but unconditional love. We laugh at some of the roles we played, but there is no sense of regret or satisfaction, of one-upmanship, or anything else. It was just the choices we made for the experiences we had."

Mother Teresa

Mother Teresa, whose reputation for gentle caring of the dying is in many ways the total opposite of Patton's, draws a similar conclusion:
"The concept [of heaven and hell] assumes so many things. It assumes first that there is judgment. Within the realm of what most people call heaven and we call Home, there is no judgment. If there is no judgment, there is no right or wrong. If there is no right or wrong, there is no sin. So, knowing now that there is no sin, knowing now that we choose the lessons that we learn, we cannot be abandoned by anybody for not doing what we thought we were going to do. Our search is always to connect to our soul, learn the lessons, and not to have to do them again."

Elvis Presley

"*Some people will probably want to know if you went to heaven or hell, and where you are now.*"
"Well, there ain't no such thing as heaven and hell. After we transition, it's just a matter of what we choose to create with our intention. At first, I chose to punish myself for what I considered the mistakes I made toward the end of my life. Finally I realized I was being used by others, and things like that. Then, with the help of some transitional folks, I began to realize who I really was."

"*'Transitional folks'—you mean spirits?*"
"Angels and other souls who provided the means of helping me to understand. It's like what the military call 'de-programming.'

"Since there are angels, isn't it heaven?"

"No, it's just unconditional love, which a lot of people consider heaven, but there's no alternative unless you put yourself there."

"Heaven implies a reward, but there's no reward?"

"There's no reward for us at Home because during our life's lessons there's nothing right and nothing wrong."

"So does everyone go Home?"

"Everyone goes Home. It's just up to them to decide what 'Home' means—the storybook heaven or hell."

Why there is no heaven or hell

It's not enough just to deny the existence of heaven and hell. We have to understand the reason *why* we can say that. This understanding comes from a knowledge of the working of the universe. The Masters explain that unconditional love does not countenance judgment of any kind. In other words, there is no place of reward nor place of punishment.

Souls coming to Earth discover that on the planet, judgment flourishes, making possible the experience of heaven and hell (on Earth and in the fourth-dimensional interface between Earth and Home). The soul needs the duality of Earth's third dimension to better understand Home's unconditional love by experiencing its opposite. It adds knowledge to the compiled wisdom of self and Source while incarnate in a physical body. The Masters say that within the universe are a number of other planets that also have souls experiencing different types of lessons. However, none of these other planets duplicates Earth's duality—the balance between negative and positive energy.

Choosing Negativity

We have seen that the mission of souls on Earth is to experience negativity in order to evaluate better the nature of unconditional love. But doing this fully involves souls' making decisions that may appear contrary to their own nature. Negativity makes itself known to us in a multitude of ways. We think of these as life lessons, and indeed, many of them are chosen by our soul prior to incarnation.

What is hard for people to understand is that we have a need created by our mission to experience negativity, which is that someone else must be the provider of that lesson. This is accomplished by our soul mates' contracting with us to be responsible for that provision. In exchange, we, in our turn, also volunteer to provide negativity. Thus, we are able to experience being, say, the abuser, as well as the abused.

Ending the assignment

So souls become abusers, control freaks, rapists, thieves, and dictators. This they do in a way similar to actors playing the roles of bad characters in a drama. The Masters said:

"The soul generally has a built-in time frame for completing its lessons. When its work is done the soul usually returns Home. If the soul has not understood the lesson within the experiences it has just finished, it may choose to take on another example within that same lifetime to see if it can understand it the next time it is presented.

"When the soul has finished and has understood all the lessons it came to learn, it may choose to return Home immediately, or use its remaining time on Earth to enter into service of other souls. If the soul enters into service, it will help other souls to understand lessons from which it has gained wisdom, lessons the others are in the midst of learning."

Returning Home

"There may be an easy transition for the soul who returns Home immediately. Or a soul may be confused and not totally aware that it is able to go Home, so it may roam around for a while, trying to maintain contact with the living.

"If a soul believes that it has led a bad life it may create whatever it interprets hell to be like, and that is where it will find itself. The eternal soul is magnificent and it can create endless versions of where it wants to be."

Every soul who incarnates on Earth will eventually return Home. Some confused souls get lost for a time but there are no exceptions.

Bertrand Russell

We spoke to Bertrand Russell's soul. He was formerly an agnostic philosopher:

"Hell is what we create for ourselves upon the planet. It does not exist otherwise. Heaven, as it is thought of by the religious organizations' authorities, also does not exist. It is not a prize to be conveyed only to those people who comport themselves with the regularities of the religion. It is a term that relates to a prize that does not exist. It is better to say that where we are in our pure form is in the presence of all that exists, from the Source to the last to be broken from the Source. And it is all equality and love; it is the essential energy of all that exists: it has no opposites, it has no polarities, it has no dualities, as found in body form. It is just a place where we return in our naked condition, where all are the same.

"You cannot do evil in soul form. You can in human form, but only so far as humans judge. The great equalizer in the human form is the judgment that the majority in society feels is correct against what the individual chooses to experience."

Adolf Hitler

If anyone knows about hell, most people think Adolf Hitler would be sure to know! Well, we interviewed the soul of Hitler. This is what he told us:

"Tell me about Satan."
"To talk about Satan is to talk about the duality of energy. Satan was chosen by the Source, by the God-Force, to be the opposite of what could be felt and perceived as the God-Force, which is unconditional love, goodness, kindness, sweetness. Satan was chosen to be the exact opposite of that: to be absolute evil, injustice, hatred. At the point of origin, Satan and the God Force are the same."

"The force of evil is a real force?"
"The opposite of the God-Force—but it only exists in the dimension of humanity. It does not exist when you come back Home."

"And hell?"
"Hell does not exist unless you create it for yourself when on the planet. Hell was the death camps."

"But when the spirits rose up from the death camps they were no longer in hell?"
"They returned to unconditional love."

123

"You've really answered this already but people ask why you did not go to hell?"

"Because I left the planet, and once I leave the physical there is no hell."

"Were you in hell when you were on Earth?"

"In my later years, very definitely, and throughout my lifetime. I was in a hell of my own making."

Dwight L. Moody

The embodiment of evil in the person of Satan was the subject of a discussion we had with the popular Christian evangelist Dwight L. Moody, who had an immense personal following during the latter part of the nineteenth century. (We noticed that he used the word God rather than Source.)

"Do you have experience of the devil?"

"I have experience of the devil in two forms: I have experience within Earth's dimension of the devil, where there is all the negativity that can possibly exist—hatred, inhumanity to others. This I have experienced on Earth, and on Earth, this energy is called the devil. Secondly, I know the core of this energy—which derives from the source of all energy, which is the Creator—is of God."

"So Satan is a fallen angel?"

"Satan is not a fallen angel. Satan is an angel who, at the request of God, became negativity, so that souls might experience the intensity of the love of God. Without an example of love's antithesis there is no true feeling within the physical of that magnificence. The energy of that negativity does not exist past the physical dimension."

"So there's no such place as hell?"
"Only on Earth."

"But there is a spiritual being who is called Lucifer or Satan?"
"He has many names. There is an energy that has been created by him, yes."

"With a regiment of minor devils, or is this a myth?"
"The energy has spread out into others so that they can tempt more people to experience this negativity—a large number of people. It would be very unlikely that there was only one soul who had to have so great a reach as to establish contact with a vast number of people. So there are, as you say, a regiment of others who have volunteered to help."

"You make it seem as if this is deliberate to give people on Earth—and only Earth—experience of negativity in all its forms."
"Yes. It is only here on Earth."

"Will that negativity ever be conquered?"
"Negativity will cease to be needed if the Earth ceases to be a cauldron of experience for souls."

"Where do people go who fear they will go to hell?"
"When they leave their body they will go to a number of different places. They will go into the unconditional love which they typify as heaven; they will go into a neutral locality because they do not allow themselves to accept heaven; they will go into a place of torment, carrying the energies of their Earth experience with them. This is torment that they hold onto and which they refuse to release. Each soul chooses its own destination, based upon the wisdom it has attained while incarnate."

"Will they ever be saved from that torment?"

"The choice is theirs: there are spirits who will help them. They can also become what you call 'discarnate souls' or 'ghosts,' when they refuse to let go of the Earth plane, even though they are no longer in physical form."

There are big differences in Moody's view now, from Home, from when he was living on Earth. Moody sees the Creator in terms of pure and unconditionally loving energy. He does not speak the language of judgment. Hell is a state of mind for those who intend to endure it. There is no hell outside the Earth's dimension. The devil, call him whatever you will, is the loyal servant of the Creator, assigned the task of causing negativity to exist on Earth as the foil for the brilliance of the light of unconditional, accepting love.

Ernest Hemingway

The novelist Ernest Hemingway was unhappy with his life. He had electric shock treatment and, seriously depressed, he committed suicide:

"When your father died you said that Catholics believe suicides go to hell. How do you now view such people?"

"In some cases it's very courageous (that is, in human terms). As a soul I know that before we come down we predetermine how we are going to live our life—not play-by-play, but the major lessons we are going to undertake. When we do that, if we get into a pattern that's not working for us, one of the possible solutions (in golf you would call it a 'mulligan'; in a soul's journey we call it a 'do-over'), you put yourself into a situation where you are back in spirit form so you can return to Earth and do it over again."

"So suicides have to re-face the tough experience they had chosen the first time?"

"If the reason they end their physical life is to start over, then yes, they have to do it all over again. Some suicides (a minority of them) are cases in which the person has made a contract to commit suicide so the family members may go through all the self-doubts and spiritual and emotional conflict that occur around a suicide."

"Do suicides go to hell?"

"Catholics say sinners go to hell, and a suicide—who has self-ended what they consider a life that will only end up in heaven or hell—go to hell. They are not correct because there is no heaven or hell. Not up here anyway. The only place where we have a heaven and a hell is upon the Earth. I experienced both while on Earth.

When on my adventures, and totally drawn by my passion, I experienced what for me was heaven on Earth because I was able to be fulfilled, to have a worth to my life, to have a passion, to have an energy. I was also in hell when I dropped into my depression. That was 'pure hell,' as they say. Nothing felt right. Nothing went right. I felt tormented, and, when medical science intervened, I was in hell.

Now that I'm in unconditional love, I can see all that happens on the planet. I can remember the things that I went through in physical form, but as long as I choose to be myself, I am in unconditional love. If I choose to re-experience the things that I did while in body form, I can create an illusion for myself of that same torment, hell, or that same bliss, my adventures."

"Then going Home to unconditional love is not really going to heaven?"

"It is much more than a human understands of heaven—where you go to the pearly gates and are greeted by Saint Peter who looks through the book and decides whether or not you have completed all of the requirements necessary to be in heaven—at which time the gates are thrown open and you are greeted down the white marble walkways by angels who float around. That's something from somebody else's novel! If you want to equate heaven with unconditional love, it is always being in perfect bliss, in a perfect understanding that all souls are connected, all souls are the same, with an interchange—you can make a choice whether to be present in a physical form or in our energetic form, which is much more comfortable. It's like being in your favorite bathrobe and slippers all the time. You don't have to worry about how you look; you just float around. That is unconditional love. There is no negative to anything."

"So is going Home not a reward for being good?"
"No, it is an entitlement for the very simple fact that you are a piece of the Creator and that you are an individual soul."

"All souls go Home?"
"All souls, regardless of what experiences they had in the physical world."

Pope John XXIII

Since Roman Catholics teach about heaven and hell and say the suicides go to hell, we thought we would raise the issue with Pope John in our interview:

"The written and oral sources currently on the planet were modified throughout the centuries to say what those in power at the time wanted them to say—particularly, going back to the time of when the Bible was put together, when the "lost" books were lost to the common people. There are several copies of the lost books, in different languages, in the basement of the Vatican. Parts of them have been leaked out recently.

"Most of the writings that are in what is now the Bible accepted by the Catholic church, were put together by the popes to give a hell-and-damnation scenario. So if the common person did not come to church, did not do what the church wanted them to do, they were damned. It was a control issue. I saw that, somewhat, while in physical form, but I did not see a way in which it could be overcome."

Carl G. Jung

The great psychologist Carl Jung also answered a question helpfully when we were discussing people living in extreme poverty and starving to death:

"This seems abominable cruelty. That so many people should die and suffer torment is hellish!"

"From a strictly physical, Earth-plane standpoint—where everything is judged good or bad, right or wrong—that would be true. From an energetic, soul-level perspective, where the soul wishes to experience different lessons, it is perfectly normal. We do not expect the mortal who is not in contact with his soul to feel and appreciate the beauty of what takes place. Each soul determines its own pathway and the means of its journey. The 'abominable cruelty' is a human judgment. Judgment does not exist at Home. Hell exists only upon the Earth."

Considering suicide

For those seriously considering suicide, a great problem is that they also feel it is an evil thing to do and they will be punished. Here are statements from the souls of two such people who told their stories to us in our book of interviews *How I Died (and what I did next)*.

First, an Indian diplomat, Jairaj, who murdered his wife and committed suicide to avoid a situation that would tarnish the family honor:

"Did people blame you for committing murder and suicide?"

"No, at Home nobody blames you. They just inquire if you've learned what you needed from the experience."

Second, Toshi, a young Japanese boy who committed suicide because he felt a failure:

"Were you criticized on the Other Side for taking your own life?"

"Oh, absolutely not, because it was part of the lessons; it was my realization that I had a choice. Considering the physical setup on Earth, had I remained, I would not have had any choices. I would have continually been in a situation where I was dominated by what was expected of me, not by any choices that I made. Once I realized I had a choice, had some power over myself, the only way I could get out of that situation was to return Home."

Sylvia Plath

Third, from *Talking with Twentieth-Century Women*, we hear from the famous American poet Sylvia Plath, who had suffered lifelong depression and, like Hemingway, had received shock therapy:

"You had attempted suicide before, and you ended your life at the age of 30 by gassing yourself in an oven. People have said Ted murdered you: Is that true or false?"

"Did he physically turn on the gas? No. Did my emotional turmoil over his not meeting my expectations play a part? A very big part. Did my interaction with the world and not thinking, because of my mental condition, that I could stand one more moment, play a part? Yes."

"Was it a long-planned suicide?"
"Suicide? Practically from my childhood suicidal thoughts were my constant companions."

"Did you, at the time, expect to have life after your death?"
"No. I simply thought, because I was not spiritual at all in that incarnation, that I would be out of my suffering."

"What actually happened to you when you died?"
"We partied as soon as I went to the Other Side. It was a matter of my having accomplished a lot, lesson-wise, during my short physical encounter, but also leaving a legacy of energy that would help many. I realized that I did not complete the lessons that I had signed up for—primarily that I would learn about myself and be able to triumph over the depression, and triumph over the control of others—so I will have to come down and experience them again. But at the same time, there were no recriminations from anybody; it was just sort of a 'Whoops! Pulled the plug a little bit too soon.'"

"You weren't censured for ending your life so early?"
"Oh, absolutely not, because a soul has freedom of choice, and the freedom of choice is at all places throughout our existence. It's when we start the lessons, how we do the lessons, if we want to re-do the lessons, when we go on to something else. There's no censure, because we're the ones who decide what we're going to do, and all we are doing—

say with a suicide—is rewriting our own script and choosing to approach it from a different direction."

"What is the purpose of taking all these lessons?"
"The purpose is to have the wisdom of them. In the realm of the soul there is nothing but unconditional love. There is no sense of emotional fulfillment, such as the satisfaction of helping another person, or the emotions that you get in loving another human, which is a romantic love, as opposed to the universal love we have. There is no experiencing the pain of a depression that you can't seem to get out of. All of those give us a sense of the magnificence of the unconditional love."

"There's no judgment?"
"Absolutely no judgment. There's simply evaluation: Did we learn enough, did we experience enough to truly appreciate and to understand and have the wisdom of that particular aspect of existence, or should we do it again?"

Taking hell with us

There is one aspect of hell that we have not dealt with so far. When a human dies, his or her soul may be strongly influenced by the life just finished. In consequence, the soul—now in that interface we call the fourth dimension, between planet Earth (the third dimension) and the celestial Home (the fifth dimension)—may be unwilling to make a move to go Home.

The reasons people have are many: their soul may not remember dying; it may want to go on controlling others left behind; it may be angry with someone and wish to have revenge; it may be frightened of future judgment; or it may imagine itself in hell.

Gerard the serial killer

We had a conversation with Gerard who believed that when he was executed he would go to hell. Here is his story. We begin while he is still alive in the body:

"What was the trial like?"

"Boring. You know, during the trial and everything else, psychiatrists would come in and decide that I was a psychotic personality, that I had no feelings whatsoever and knew what was right and wrong but just didn't care, and that I was a sociopath, which was, I guess, a pretty good description of me.

"All this time, I was also getting preached to by the 'gossip' people—you know, by the gospel people—how I was going to go to hell and how I was going to burn for all eternity for everything I did. All of the families of these prostitutes [whom he had murdered] came out of the woodwork to tell me how, you know, I was going to be damned and all—so I began to envision what it was going to be like. And it started out being like my childhood. But then it started taking on different characteristics: of fire that burned but didn't burn you, and all kinds of just horrible, horrible things. So by the time I got to the point of them giving me the needle [to execute him], I was sure that I was going to hell."

"Were any of the preachers trying to convert you to believing in Christianity?"

"Not really. There wasn't anybody who really liked me. And I think it had a lot to do with the fact that I wasn't very pleasant to any of them when they came in. So it turned out that everybody was condemning me. The night that I was to end my existence, they put the needle in and I awoke in complete darkness, and I knew that I was on my way to hell.

I didn't want to move, but then I felt myself being drawn forward, so I just gave in to this pressure that was pulling me."

"Were you aware that you were outside of your body?"
"I don't know if I made the connection of being outside of my body. I knew I wasn't in the prison. I knew that I was no longer in that physical body, but I didn't know if I was a body. I could see something that was like a body because I envisioned that I would have a body when I went to hell."

"Yes, go on."
"And then I began to feel the heat. And I began to hear the shrieks of people in torment."

"That you'd been taught to expect?"
"Which was what I had accepted would be the norm for somebody like me."

"But you didn't see them? You just felt and heard them?"
"I just felt and heard things. There then began to be vibrations like fire. When I was a truck driver, you could see the heat rise off the pavement during the day, you know, in vapors. And I saw that, but I saw it in red, all round me. And I was consumed by this intense heat that was constantly there, eating away at everything. It was clogging my mind so that I couldn't think, and I felt at that time it was what I deserved for what I had been."

"Were you aware of the passage of time?"
"Not really, because everything was the same. I mean, there were the shrieks, there was the torment, there was the unending quality of it. There was the inability to think, the inability to be comfortable, the inability to even give another

person difficulty as I had done all my life. There was a solitariness that was worse than anything else."

"But without a body, you couldn't feel pain? Or did you imagine pain?"
"I imagined pain. I imagined myself being burned, being scalded. I imagined my head being eaten up from the inside out by all these horrible screams, and it got to the point where I began screaming because of the misery I was feeling. And underlying all of it was this thought: 'This is what you have earned for yourself.' Just as my mother used to beat me if I didn't get out of the house fast enough, this was what I deserved for not being attentive to what was going on; this was what I deserved for having taken the lives of so many people."

"How did that come to an end?"
"For the longest time I was shutting out as much as I could, so that I didn't have to listen to it, didn't have to feel it. And then one day it was almost as if I got tired of putting in all of the effort to shut it out. And I said, 'Fine. I know this is supposed to be eternal, but maybe if I just open myself to it, it will consume me and that will be the end.' So I relaxed as much as I could. And, of course, the pain seemed to become more intense, the screaming more piercing, but inside the screaming was a little voice that said, 'Are you ready now to accept yourself?' I had no idea what it meant so I shut everything down again. And then some period of time later, I opened up again and there was an even sweeter voice that said, 'This isn't who you really are.'

"At this time something began deep inside of me, almost a recognition. I didn't know who it was, but I decided I would listen. And then there was a whole group of them who began to tell me that I was creating this hell that I was in. Being a soul (which was what made me eternal), was

135

what allowed me to exist after leaving my human body. They insisted that I was eternal, and that as an eternal soul, I could create what I wanted. Of course, I didn't believe it, you know. It was just some other do-gooder trying to help me.

"Then the sweet voice came back again and it said, 'Just try to turn down the heat a little. You can do it.' So I thought, 'Hey, let's give it a shot, because being in 120-degree heat all the time just isn't my thing. I'm a mountain boy.' So I said, 'Okay, heat down,' and it got cooler. Then a voice came and said, 'Shut out the other shrieks. Shut out the other tormented souls.' That was a little harder, but I gradually was able to, and I think it was by going inside of myself that I was able to shut out the shrieks. And then slowly, slowly, everything that I had thought I deserved—the fires, the shrieks, the misery, the pain—was gone."

"What was left?"

"Darkness. Darkness was what was left, and I was alone, and I didn't hear the voices for a while. And so I said to them, 'Ok, I certainly don't want this darkness.' And they said, 'Well then, change it. Change it to what you want.' And I said, 'Well, I want to have... I want to be in the mountains. I want to be in the fresh air.' And I was immediately on my favorite mountaintop. And I said, 'Well does this mean that I'm alive again?' And they said, 'No. This means your soul can create for itself what it feels it deserves.' And I said, 'But I was such a horrible person!' And they said, 'Yes, in that lifetime, by the standards of society, you were a horrible person. But you chose to experience that. It was just a part in a play that you assigned yourself. That is not who you are.' And I said, 'What? What do you mean?' And they said, 'You are like us. You are part of the Creator. You are part of the Source of everything. We are your friends.' I said, 'I don't have any friends.' They said, 'We are your soul friends. You didn't have any physical friends in that lifetime. That was one of the characteristics of the role that you had in that play.'

"Did it take you a long time to believe in what they were saying?"
"Well, there is no time at Home. But if you were to put it against Earth time, it was several years of very slowly remembering, of being able to peel off all the layers, the insulation I had placed around myself during my role playing as Gerard so that I could get down to the essence of who I was."

"So you began to realize that you were a soul?"
"I began to accept it because I could feel it—that I was a soul, that I was the same as they. We had one tremendous party when I finally came Home. It was like the reborn individual shucking all of the shackles, all of the layers that had hidden his true essence. And I am now, as they, totally aware of myself. I have now understood the lessons I learned as Gerard."

Summary

We need to have a revolution in our thinking to abandon the familiar concepts of heaven and hell as future destinations for our soul. The reality of life at Home is that *all* souls live equally in an energetic dimension quite different from that of our polarized planet. It is a realm of unconditional love, the basic energetic substance of the universe.

Hell has no part in that energetic dimension because Home is devoid of all judgment. Hell is a this-world, present state of mind which we may create within our human self, or which may be thrust upon us while we live on the planet. In no way is hell a dire future punitive incarceration, divinely ordained as retribution for our sins (such as is perceived about suicide), because Source is non-judgmental. Hell exists only within the energetic dimension of planet Earth.

Likewise, heaven is simply a present state of mind found within our earthly experience, because Home, although suffused with unconditional love, in no way exists as judgment's place of celestial reward for our being good and doing good. Every soul who incarnates on Earth will eventually return Home. There are no exceptions. Good and evil, as we know them in our human existence, belong solely to the ethics of our polarized planet. These concepts lose their relevance for our eternal soul when it frees itself from our human body.

Homosexuality

Introduction

To say that the issue of human homosexuality is an age-old problem feels like an understatement. In the face of social opposition, homosexuals' careers have been ruined, their families split asunder, their relationships wrecked. Many have committed suicide in despair, some have been killed in hatred—the account of misery caused by other people's rejection of a large part of the Gay, Lesbian, Bisexual, and Transgender (GLBT) population seems endless.

The purpose of this essay is not to add to the usual discussion of homosexuality and homophobia—there are many people better able to do that for you. Our purpose is to bring a cosmic viewpoint to the issue, through the teaching and opinion of senior guides and individual souls on the Other Side who have made their observations in frequent communications with us.

This is also not the moment to discuss the merits of metaphysical communication. As we have said earlier, we understand and respect skepticism, and we accept that not everyone will be prepared to believe in the authenticity and reliability of channeled messages (even those coming through as sound a channel as Toni Ann Winninger is widely acknowledged to be). Skeptics are invited to suspend final judgment on this essay until they have examined its content. The context is our communication with the Masters and other invited souls: take it or leave it. We begin with an overview of gender as a spiritual experience.

Souls and Gender

The Masters write: "Do souls have a sexually significant gender? (That is: are they either male or female, a male-female hybrid, or sexless?) No. What you understand as a person's sex is part of the duality of planet Earth. Outside of the dimension of Earth there is no duality, no opposites, so no sexual differences. A soul has the characteristics that are emotionally considered to be male or female on Earth—all in one package.

"Since a soul has all of that which you consider to be the characteristics of both sexes together in a single container, the energetic feelings of any portion of that container are both male and female. If channels access your female energy they will think you are female. If they access your male energy they will swear you are male—yet you are energetically both. At Home, you are a soul without a specific sexual designation but with all of the feelings that enable you to play either role, as you choose, whenever you come to Earth.

"When you decided to make a trip to planet Earth, you didn't do it on the spur of the moment with no thought or planning beforehand. You researched the things you wanted to experience within the duality of Earth, and what you would most like to learn. These situations are called 'life lessons.' You queried your advisors—your council of twelve souls who had studied the same types of lessons before you, and your various soul mates. Only then did you decide what you wanted to do. The lessons you chose are the purposes you have in incarnating and then reincarnating."

The dualistic world

Souls come to planet Earth for a purpose, to experience negativity in a celestial classroom that has been uniquely designated for the purpose:

"Earth was created to be different from every other physical location. Its appeal to the learning process of the soul is its polarity. The soul's choice to come to Earth is to experience life within a polarity, or state of negativity, that cannot be found anywhere else.

"Each soul does not choose to experience everything, all in one lifetime. Things may be occurring on the planet when they are there, but souls will not participate in any more than they are capable of learning from at a particular time. Your soul may prefer to go to other places than Earth to have a life. Even within this polarity you may have plenty of happiness upon Earth, if you complete the lessons you came to learn and remember your true nature—which is unconditional love. Home is a place of continuous love. Duality exists only on planet Earth."

Choice of parents, gender, gifts

"Having completed the decisions about whatever life lessons it wants to experience, a soul starts considering the stage setting for the drama. It looks around and decides what type of parents will facilitate its goals and also considers whether the parents' own journey would benefit from having it as a child. So it makes a contract with them.

"Next, what gender will make it easy or difficult to accomplish the soul's plans? (Gender may complicate or facilitate some lessons, such as being female in a male-dominated society, or being GLBT—homosexual.) The soul asks itself if gender is a major or minor aspect of its human life. Decisions are made accordingly."

Judy Garland

Our first witness on the gender issue is the film star and singer Judy Garland whom we interviewed recently. Sexually, Judy was straight in that lifetime. She paints a basic and simple overview of the gender issue from her perspective:

"So you have had lives as a man as well as a woman?"
"Yes."

"Do you feel yourself to be a woman or a man, now you are back Home?"
"I am everything that I have been. Wherever my concentration is I would be what you consider either male or female."

"But at the root of things you are neither male nor female."
"That's correct.

Ernest Hemingway

Hemingway was clearly bisexual. His testimony raises the frequently stated idea that people have made a conscious decision to be gay, and can be talked out of it. Hemingway himself clearly lived on a knife-edge between his acceptance of homosexuality and his homophobia toward gay people.

"Many of your works allude to sexual ambiguities and destructive relationships between men and women. Grace, your mother, dressed you early on as a girl, calling you Ernestine. Later in your life F. Scott Fitzgerald's wife, Zelda,

accused him of having a homosexual affair with you, but you often acted and wrote in a homophobic way. Can you shed light on your sexuality?"

"I would say it was everything for everybody. My mother dearly wanted a girl so my early times were patterned after those of a young girl. It was not until I began going to school that I got into a feeling for the sexes. The gentleness of the female, that my mother shared with me early on, never left me. To combat that I also sought out the most robust [brave, adventurous deeds] a male would have. I tasted and experienced all of the possibilities that one may choose while in physical form. But I will not tell of my dalliances and alliances; that is for my partners to divulge if they choose. Needless to say I fully utilized the body I had, and enjoyed all the pleasures it made possible."

Elvis Presley

Hemingway was not alone in his confusion. The young Elvis Presley was also very highly protected by his mother, and had such confusion that, although he did actually marry and father a child, his sexuality now appears under-developed:

"As a mama's boy you were very shy and isolated at first. You seem to have been passionate about girls, not just in high school, and not only in your relationships with Dixie, Anita, June, Natalie, Connie, Ann-Margret, Linda, your wife Priscilla, and your fiancée Ginger, but also a number of young teenage girls. Can you explain the nature of your sexuality?"

"I was very confused by my sexuality. Being extremely protected, I never got social skills when I was young, concerning dealing with the sexes. When I started being adored by girls it was sorta as if my mama was there with me, and the affection that she always lavished on me was coming from outside sources. So it was multiplying and was

143

very comfortable to me. I really got into that particular groove. In the beginning it didn't have anything to do with sex; it had to do with how I felt about myself. The image I had of myself was that I was shy and didn't have experience. Then to go out and be *adored* by people gave me a definition of who I was—who I was as this person everybody liked, everybody wanted to be with. It didn't go into sexual things until much, much later, because my whole sexual identity was kinda confused."

"Eventually, did you have sex with minor girls?"
"Not all the way to intercourse, no. It mainly came to the point of liking to have them around because they adored me. I was 'The King' and what was important to me was how I felt about myself."

"In your last years there seemed to be a confusion in your sexuality because in concerts you began to look, dress, and act like Liberace. Were you ever actually bisexual or just confused?"
"Totally confused. I did have some cuddling time with males, but it never went much beyond that. I gravitated toward anybody who could make me feel good."

Andy Warhol

Those who think homosexuality must be something to do with the mother's attitude, may need to hear from Andy Warhol, a self-acknowledged gay man:

"Was your mother accepting of your homosexuality?"
"My mother accepted me exactly as I was. She did not make any distinctions one way or the other between my lifestyle and the lifestyle of my siblings."

"Did you choose to be homosexual before coming to planet Earth?"

"I chose to experience ambivalence, which was the period of time before I accepted and told others that I was in fact homosexual. It was a constant battle of: am I doing this to be different? am I doing this because I'm actually being accepted by a male partner rather than a female partner? or am I doing it because that is what my body and my mind need at this time? I did put all of those patterns together for something I wished to experience in this lifetime. "

Gender

Now let's bring in the Masters to give us an overview of the issue as seen from the perspective of the celestial Home:

"When is gender decided upon?"

"The decision concerning gender is made before the joining of egg and sperm."

"How about differences of sexual orientation and transsexuality?"

"Those are all lessons the soul wishes to experience."

"So sexual orientation is the lesson?"

"Yes."

"How does it come about? Is it that the soul is now wanting to be the other sex?"

"That's only how it is manifested. Souls wish to experience ambivalence, prejudice, and self-worth issues generally. It goes further than that in their ability to clearly feel themselves in the physicality of the body. In feeling the physicality of the body, souls begin to re-feel their own essence.

"Primarily, souls come down to learn lessons, and then, while in the process of learning, or after having learned those lessons, to recall the essence of who they are. So people who are going through an apparent conflict between whatever their physical body shows everyone else, and whatever their inner feelings may be, are actually leaning toward connecting with who each of them is as a soul, as opposed to who they are as a physical being."

"Is a gay male truly in a male body with an emotional desire to be a female?"

"It is other than that. It is that they are able to tap into their emotional core, which is sexless. They choose to experience what it is that makes them feel better in a human body, which are the emotions and the energy of the female aspects of themselves. Because society says that makes them female, they identify strongly with that gender, which makes them feel so good that then they choose to be female, or to play the female role while remaining in the male body."

"Can homosexuals be talked out of their attitude by society?"

"If they choose not to continue to grow, experience, and learn lessons, yes, they can. But in that case they wall themselves off and fail to continue to grow and to mature."

"So a gay's not a hard-wired female in a male body, but a soul tapping into its female nature more than its male nature, and who happens to be in a male body?"

"Yes."

Now for case studies:

Barbara Jordan

We start with the lesbian Barbara Jordan, who was elected to the US Congress from the State of Texas and made her mark in the political arena as a wise and thoughtful orator:

"On a camping trip, a year or two before going to Washington, DC, you met your partner, Nancy Earl. You both kept your lesbian relationship a secret for 20 years. Was your joint silence to protect you from political discrimination?"

"At that time there was only one thing worse than being a black southerner, and that was being homosexual. My word, my message, my mission would have been totally ignored and unimportant, because the only thing people would have seen was an aberration in nature, which was how homosexuality was thought of at that time. I would have been condemned by mainstream society, by all the religious organizations, and by the political parties, as something that detracted from their mission."

"You said, 'There is no way that I can equate discrimination on the basis of sexual preference with discrimination on the basis of skin color.' Did you mean that being a lesbian involved making a sexual preference rather than being homosexually hard-wired from birth?"

"That wasn't what I meant by the statement. The statement was that there were things that could be excused of a person because society believed they had no choice. Society did believe, in some realms, that homosexuality was a choice, so to that degree, yes, that was what I meant. To a larger degree, I meant that all blacks were lumped together as just being the progeny of slaves and of people who were lesser. Homosexuals at that time (and to this day by some religions) were considered to be evil, abnormal, a threat energetically to anyone who came in contact with them, almost as if we had a virus that was contagious. A leper is a perfect example."

"But is the homosexual hard-wired—in other words, it isn't a personal preference but something that you have to do?"
"How you perceive it depends upon the lesson that you came down to experience. If a person's lesson is to experience homosexuality, with all of the condemnations of society and dealing with all the lessons of being hated and considered outcasts from society, being considered crazy, evil, then, yes, it is 'hard-wired' and a part of you from the very beginning of that lifetime.

"It may, however, also appear to be a choice that one makes because one energetically connects with a member of the same sex but cannot energetically connect with someone of the opposite sex, so it becomes a choice as to how to spend the majority of one's life. People may deny their feelings and enter a heterosexual marriage, or they may lead dual lives. Your wording of 'hard-wiring' implies only that it was a part of the plan decided before incarnation with no way to deny the tendency. I differentiate in that souls may choose to hide from their feelings even if they had planned to have that as a lesson."

If a GLBT orientation relates to a choice we made prior to incarnating on planet Earth, remember that the lesson is rarely of sexuality but of ambivalence. Sexual orientation will be *how* the psychological lesson is presented to the soul, rather than the soul's choice of gender.

James Baldwin

In our second case study we see the race issue, which Barbara Jordan raised, being explored by James Baldwin, a gifted African-American writer:

"In your novels Another Country *and* Tell Me how Long the Train's been Gone, *the characters are straight, gay, and bisexual. How early on did you become aware of your homosexuality and how would you describe yourself?"*

"Very early on I became aware of homosexuality because my stepfather was a homophobe. One of the neighbors was gay, so it was a topic on which we were *preached at* concerning him. I would describe myself as an experimenter—sometimes just to see what was there, and sometimes being forced there out of rebellion."

"How did your mother react to your gay lifestyle?"

"My mother had a certain fear that my stepfather would kill me, would beat me to death."

"What is the soul seeking to achieve in the advance choice it makes of gender and sexual orientation?"

"Basically, with gender, the soul is trying to experience all the things that society envisions concerning a particular gender. With sexual leanings, if it is a heterosexual one, the idea is to be able to marry together all of the energies that are possible between two people of opposite sexes. You take together two people leaning toward totally different types of emotions and different types of ways to handle everyday situations.

"When it comes to homosexual tendencies, this chosen experience can be for any of several different reasons. It can be selected to deal with all of society's reactions to what homosexuality means, or it can be chosen to be able to further identify oneself within that particular sex by having a partner who is like a role model for you. It's a very close relationship that allows you to compare notes, so to speak: 'I'm having these problems; how do you solve them?' 'What are your feelings when you get a reaction from outside a certain type?' There are all kinds of reactions and situations

149

that come to you, and those are, or they encompass, the various reasons that you choose a particular sex, a particular lifestyle, a particular sexual orientation."

"Your second novel, Giovanni's Room, *was explicitly sexual. Why did you choose a cast of white characters for that story?"*

"It was a little bit of fun, and I chose whites because, had I chosen blacks, the entire race would have been typecast by the book. People who were white, or of other races that had not had much dealing with blacks, would have believed that all blacks were the same. Because whites come from so many different places—whether it be eastern Europe, the United States, Canada—readers could get the idea that I was discussing particular tendencies and yearnings that some people had, which were not specific to a race."

"In your next two novels you showed a change of direction. In Another Country *and* Tell Me How Long the Train's Been Gone, *racial and sexual issues abound..."*

"I was hoping with those books to show to people who were reading them simply because they had read my former book [*Giovanni's Room*] that there were not a lot of differences between the races, except for the fact that blacks were truthful in what they did. They were not hypocritical. They did not take their sexuality and close the door and hide it. They lived the way they felt they needed to. They weren't puritanical because that's not the way the human animal is."

"Do you now see the link between sexuality and racism quite as strongly as you did then?"

"No, not at all. I do see that blacks are still more truthful. Basically blacks, if they are not in positions where they are competing with whites, such as white collar workers, are true to themselves and their feelings in the way they express themselves in all matters including sexuality. Whereas the whites, if they are in higher echelons where they feel they are on a pedestal and must be honored and obeyed, keep their sexual tendencies hidden behind the closet door. More of the whites, the normal Joes, the ones who are not out there on pedestals, are beginning to have the same feeling and exhibit the same tendencies toward sexuality as the blacks. This is the normal, healthy human response to sexuality.

"So then we had the disparity of the blacks being overtly sexual and the whites being repressed. We now have some of the blacks being repressed to fit into white society, and we have some of the whites finding they don't have to be repressed because of what they do or how their family is viewed within society. They relish being true to themselves and their feelings."

Oscar Wilde

We also interviewed Oscar Wilde, one of the most notable gay men in recent history, who was actually bisexual. He was very psychic as a boy, very controlled by his snobbish mother, very artistic, and a brilliant playwright. Reference is made in this passage of Wilde's homosexual affair with Lord Alfred (Bosie) Douglas, for which Wilde was imprisoned for "gross indecency."

"There were conflicts during your life over sexuality. I have two quotes: from The Duchess of Padua, *'We are each our own devil, and we make this world our hell,' and from* An Ideal Husband, *'Life is never fair...and perhaps it is a good thing for most of us that it is not.' Which is the better evaluation of your affair with Bosie, and your incarceration in Reading jail for the crime of gross indecency?"*

"I was simply following my physical energies, my physical needs that I felt unable to ignore. Because they were so strong I found it to be very unjust that I was condemned for them, but that was because I did not fit into the little cubby-hole which was expected of each proper gentleman. We were also a bit glib about the whole situation, and uncaring of the consequences."

"You were a married man with two sons who were born in quick succession after your marriage. Was your homosexuality, especially your liaison with young male prostitutes, a selfish disregard of morality, or—as some have suggested—a search for self-identity? Did you attempt to live without a soul?"

"It is very difficult now totally to comprehend everything I did when in physical form. It is so different from the way I feel now. I was tormented by physical needs, which, after the birth of my children, were not relieved by my wife. At first I thought I would go by way of the prostitute, as did many at that time. But then I discovered the beauty of the young male body. The first encounter was actually a seduction of me."

"At Oxford?"
"Yes."

"Did the homosexual seduction predate marriage to Constance?"
"It did, but it was an embarrassment to me and something I tried to hide until I found that the common way of man and woman would not work for me. I tried to blot out the feelings I had had in the first encounter, and to make them disappear, by becoming normal within the realm of sexual relations. When I was denied those experiences, at first I did get enough release to be satisfied in the marriage. But after the second child, Constance, not wanting any more

children, forbade me her bed. Then in my sadness, as I went out wandering, I was reacquainted with beauty. Constance became for me the epitome of the hag—that person from whose constant pecking one wants to free oneself. I found relief in the gentleness of beings who wanted to share— young male prostitutes—who did not wish to control, did not wish to peck, did not wish to direct, and who wished only to have money in exchange for pleasuring."

"What part does morality play in that drama?"
"That was where I convinced myself that I was cutting myself off from my soul, and without the soul I surmised I did not have to worry about condemnation or repercussions. I was simply going to live in the physical and not have to worry about anything beyond."

"You are describing your sexuality as having such force that you could not control it except by taking up homosexuality. It wasn't a confusion; it was your deliberate choice."
"It was a choice, a physical drive, and an obsession with me. It came at a time when I was totally inexperienced, and led by another to feel the release, to feel physical closeness to another being without other agendas (the pressures of taking care of the house, providing for the servants). It was just the act itself. When I was forbidden Constance's bed, and needed release, had I gone to another woman I felt that I would still have had those same female pressures—a family/no family. I found instead in males a companionship, a camaraderie, all wrapped round the ability for sexual release—but with no ties."

"In this generation on Earth, there is a point of view expressed strongly by critics that seems to support what you are saying—that homosexuality is a deliberate choice and you can be talked out of it. How do you view that attitude?"

"I have two opinions of what you have just said. I believe that in most cases it is a deliberate choice in the present age, the choice of how to experience closeness and sexual relationships. I do not feel it is something people can be talked out of, if their sense of self, if their ability to sense love and vibration within a close personal relationship is attuned to one of the same sex. There still is a choice to participate in that relationship, because everything on Earth is 'freedom of choice.' People can either follow the urges they have or deny them, but they cannot be talked out of their urges. It has to be their own choice whether or not to follow up on the urge to partake in a physical encounter."

"Do you regret the Bosie affair, or did you learn from it?"
"I don't regret anything that I experienced. Everything provided lessons."
"What was the nature of the Bosie affair lesson?"
"First, if you are in human form and in society, you must be conscious of societal rules and regulations. Second, no man anywhere in physical form lives on an island alone, and is unaffected by others. There are consequences when you choose to go beyond accepted behavior, if you remain within society. For a while I thought that as I had chosen to separate myself from what I considered moral repercussions for what I was doing, that that would create around me an island where I could exist, do as I chose, and not impact others or be impacted by them. My largest lesson was that I could not."

The Masters' commentary

"Masters, In view of your remarks about homosexuality, will you comment on Oscar's remark that he was thwarted in his heterosexuality and, having an excess of sexual drive, he was

driven into homosexuality? It was not a sexual confusion, or soul searching, but a deliberate choice."

"Oscar Wilde was a bisexual, not a true homosexual, in that particular human incarnation. He engaged in and was able to get his physical release within both forms of sexuality. It was opportunity that directed where he went. His feelings and convictions were of what to him was more pleasurable and safer. He was a man who feared being dominated by anyone. Part of the domination he felt came through anything female, so it was then his choice to express his sexuality primarily with males. It was not confusion but a life lesson that he was experiencing; it was a conscious choice. The majority of those in human form who are homosexual are dealing with energies, coming from within them from their soul, which make them resonate only with souls who are physically in the same sexual body as they are."

"So bisexuality is a different type of experience?"
"In most cases."

"What about transsexuality?"
"Transsexuality is a state of internal confusion so pervasive that the person cannot resonate with the body they are in. They go through a series of life lessons—several incarnations or a number of life lessons within one lifetime, such as: they are born male, they are raised male, although their feelings are always feminine to the extent that they are not satisfied with being a male acting in a feminine relationship with another male. Their feelings are so strong that they have to become physically female themselves in order to feel as they should feel. So there is a difference."

"How do you view homophobia?"

155

"A homophobe is a person who is aware of both masculine and feminine energies within themselves and fears that they may be different from their friends because of the yearnings or the sensations they have. It is normal for a person to be able to sense all such feelings. Because they may feel a strong pull toward someone of the same sex, they rebel against it to the extent that they become raving condemners—of 'girly-men.'"

Margaret Mead

We draw our survey of the question of homosexuality to a close, aware that we have not dealt with the 1001 issues you may want to raise, but with two comments on the central points made from the Other Side. First, a comment from the anthropologist Margaret Mead, noted for her book on sexuality in Samoa:

"Can you say now what are desirable norms for human sexuality?"
"I think that has to be determined by each individual person. It has to be determined by the pathway that that soul is walking upon in the physical life now being experienced. We cannot say for other souls what is right or wrong or *normal* for that matter, in a third-dimensional way, for them. Souls are here to learn the lessons they choose, and those may have sexual aspects to them that are not what society thinks is normal."

"So there's no norm for society as a whole?"
"No, because if you are experiencing the lesson of frigidity, or you are experiencing the lesson of promiscuity, both of them are perfectly normal for that lifetime. If you are experiencing a mastership of your body, where (even while being bathed in sexually explicit things) you wish to be

celibate to increase the energy within you so that you can use that to, say, preach, that is normal as well. Whatever is the path of the individual soul is normal for that soul."

Conflicts and the soul

The Masters: "On a soul level we do not judge things to be 'good' or 'bad.' That does not mean that your soul while incarnate on the planet cannot sense the energy of society in judging things that way. But it also means that a soul has the choice *not* to get involved in things outside its lesson plan. Such a non-interactive choice is not to be confused with refusing to be concerned or absolving oneself from any blame for not jumping into the fray.

"The soul cannot have the full human experience unless it has an aspect of self that is ego-based. If the soul remained completely bathed in unconditional love it could experience nothing. Some of the lessons that a soul chooses to learn deal with an interaction in the physical and emotional traumas impacting other people. However, many soul lessons involve only the souls' personal interactions with those around them.

"When the soul lesson involves a larger group of players, this may lead to an investment of time and money to support one side or another in a conflict, actively protesting the actions of one group, or even diving physically into the conflict on behalf of one party. These must be the tests along the soul's path or they become a diversion and will slow down the soul's journey to wisdom. Some souls become so involved in this fashion they do not face the challenges they came to Earth to complete.

"Remember, each soul makes its own choices. One soul cannot make choices for another. To get entwined in a conflict, speak out about it, or protest the actions of a group may be part of a lesson in self-worth, or a recognition of your own power, or a refusal to be controlled by another, or even the experience of getting sucked up in a group hysteria.

"Whatever the true reason for a soul's activity, the worth may be evaluated by going inside and asking, 'Why am I doing this? What do I seek to gain myself out of this action?' If the answer has to do with a lesson or emotion you are trying to understand, it is part of your journey. If the answer is to 'show' those people, examine your motives because you are mirroring something you need to face about yourself."

~ * ~

Life Lessons

I. Overview

Source and Earth

When considering questions concerning life lessons, people must be clear about the starting point. The Masters teach that Source is unequivocally composed of unconditional love, but that being of a pure essence, it was unable to measure its own magnificence. To make such an assessment possible it was necessary to create an opposing energy, one that is not unconditional love, with which Source essence might be compared. For this task Source did two things:

First, locating it on planet Earth, Source created a self-contained environment of duality, half of which was positive energy and half negative energy. The planet, which the Masters sometimes call "the duality," is unique. There is no other part of the universe designated to be like it.

Second, Source broke off billions of individual souls to live in the duality, experiencing and comparing both positive and negative experiences on behalf of the whole energy of Source.

The purpose of this controlled experiment is to permit a comparison between positive and negative energies to be made by those souls choosing to incarnate on Earth. This comparison is a "hands on" activity as the souls, as particles of Source, discover for themselves the difference between negative energy and their own essence, unconditional love.

It is not an imposition made on souls to do their "duty" to an almighty ruler, but a common activity willingly entered into for the benefit of the whole, to discover the true nature of unconditional love, the essence of the whole. For this reason, one of the laws of the universe confirms the complete freedom of choice exercised by all souls at all times, both while working in the dimension of Home, and also while living incarnate on the planet.

Experience and wisdom

Our spiritual guides make a clear distinction between knowledge and wisdom. We may see on television or read descriptions in books of archeologists searching for remains of lost civilizations. Their work is painstaking! They may be down on their knees in the hot sun for hours, brushing the desert sand with a soft brush, working to uncover a fragile, ancient, decorative pot or piece of bone. Watching the television program we may pick up some knowledge of the archeological dig, but that is not the same as being there. The archeologist working with the brush under the hot sun has more than a distant view. What is gained on the site of the dig is the wisdom of personal experience—when people can say, "I was there." The difference between knowledge and wisdom is that wisdom is being able to apply our initial broad understanding to other situations because we have gone to a deeper level by what we have actually done.

Although the akashic record in the celestial database carries knowledge—details of everything known in the universe—the soul seeks to go deeper into its experiences and bring back hands-on wisdom to benefit Source energy's search for self-knowledge. When it comes to life lessons, it is wisdom rather than mere knowledge that is desired.

The Masters give this example: "Let's just say that you live in a land where it is hot and sunny every day. You think this is marvelous but admit that it is a bit boring to have the same monotonous weather day after day. One day you move to the South Pole with its sub-zero temperatures, winds that threaten to remove your coat, and blowing ice that obscures the sun. Then you really know what you have lost! Had you not chosen to go and experience something different on Earth, you would never fully realize the perfection of Home."

Positive and negative experience

Souls come from the environment of unconditional love. So, if they wanted to study in a loving place they would not need to travel down to planet Earth. No, their purpose is to experience negative situations in order to compare them with their own loving essence. Because the soul uses duality (+/-) to evaluate any experience and to know its worth, the only way it can add knowledge to the compiled wisdom of self and Source is to be incarnate in a physical body on the planet designed to provide it.

The soul as an actor

One metaphor for the work of the incarnate soul sees the soul as being like an actor. Human life is a character played on the world's stage. The character may be powerful or weak, easily tempted or resilient. Not only that, but the playwright may have needed a member of the cast to play a truly negative role—taken perhaps from human history, or religious myth. The actor studies the lines and learns to play the moves; then on the night of the play the audience sees someone who is thoroughly negative—beating, maiming, or killing other characters on stage. The curtain falls and the audience leaves the theatre. Backstage all the actors in their dressing rooms are removing their makeup and changing into their everyday clothes. At home the actor who took the "evil" part may be a loving family man, or a woman who is currently deeply involved in caring for an aging mother. Metaphors don't tell us everything, but we may be helped by thinking of the soul as taking different roles to experience negativity either as the perpetrator of the incident or as the victim. Seen from the soul's perspective, there is no good or evil, right or wrong—there are roles to play that provide experience from which the soul may gather the wisdom of that negativity.

Preparing for a life on Earth

The Masters continue: "When you decided to make a trip to planet Earth, which we call incarnation, you didn't do it on the spur of the moment with no thought or planning beforehand. You researched all the possible things you wanted to experience within the duality of Earth, and what you most wanted to learn. These situations are called life lessons. You queried your advisors—your council of twelve souls who had studied the same types of lessons before you, and your various soul mates. Only then did you decide what you wanted to do. The lessons you chose are the purposes you have in incarnating and then reincarnating.

"To ensure that you would experience these desired lessons, you made contracts with other souls to help you set up the necessary staging for the events. Some of the incidents would be considered as positive in the human realm and others as negative. Your purpose was to figure out what you wished to learn and then, in understanding it, find the wisdom beneath that could be applied to all other events in your soul's continuing lifetimes.

"The one purpose you *always* incarnate with is to find what it is that you wanted to accomplish. If we told you the specifics of each lesson you had decided to learn, you would be missing half the process. When you were in school, if the teacher had only given you the answers to questions without first asking the questions, you would have learned nothing. For us to tell you the purpose you had in mind would be the same. So we say that discovering your purpose *is* your purpose.

"'What is my purpose in coming here?' is a frequently asked question. Most people seem to think that if they are unaware of their purpose in life, they are doing something wrong. Let us repeat one of our mantras: 'Nothing is right or wrong.' And another: 'You are always exactly where you need to be to learn the lessons you sought.'

"To know what it is like to be controlled by another, we have many different choices, slavery being one. For many of you, slavery brings to mind what happened in the Americas, where a group of entrepreneurs went to poor nations, kidnapped people there, and forced them into servitude. Slavery is only one form of personal control exercised over another, the taking away of what an individual soul believes to be its freedom of choice. Adult control may be exercised when a parent refuses to let her child choose a favored course of study at school, or engage in an after-school activity.

"A control situation frequently happens within your families when a child expresses an interest in a particular sport—tennis, soccer, or football. The parents think ambitiously and when their offspring shows talent, they become like masters dictating that, because the child is so proficient, he must continue to practice, even though he may not wish to continue the experience. So there are early morning practices, and then more practices, and body-building, and a forced nutritional regime, all much beyond what the child ever sought to have. That sort of control is a type of slavery.

"How does this equate with the lessons we mentioned at the start? The soul has chosen to experience being controlled and giving up responsibility and freedom of choice to another. It may have given up control to avoid having to think or to be responsible for what happens.

"Can this soul learn anything in that scenario? The simple answer is that it can learn only if it realizes that it really does have a choice and can change the direction of its life by backing out of the agreement to be enslaved or, in the sports example, by taking responsibility and telling the parents, 'I do not choose to do that.' The slave in chains may escape, as many did. The indentured person may fulfill the contract and then move immediately to another location.

"Escape can be physical, mental, emotional, or by going Home—death. Many times when a soul, having experienced being controlled, is given the opportunity to move into a position where it is in charge of its own life, the fear of having to be responsible for itself keeps it in the same situation and it does not choose to move on.

"The lesson for the soul is to recognize what it is doing in this lifetime, what it has experienced, and how it has the freedom of choice to learn not to be controlled by others. It can also recognize that it can make decisions and move from fear into acceptance of itself as an individual. Then it can finish the lesson by assuming responsibility for itself, heading off the control of another, and then advancing to the next chosen lesson.

"Similar teaching experiences include souls having to rely on other people. They may also involve aspects of illness where, because of despair over their situation, people cut off the energy flow through their body and become critically ill. (They have the ability, if they go inside themselves, to learn that they can with their intention reverse the blockages they have created.)

"Each of these experiences constitutes a lesson. Unless your soul taps your inner knowledge to find the basic experience you wish to have, and then completes it, you will not gain the wisdom of that experience—and you may need to choose to return with a different example of the same lesson in that present or a future life experience, until you have finally mastered it."

Why are we here?

"When you get ready to come down to Earth to learn some life lessons, you get to decide which ones you wish to encounter. These can be such things as anger, betrayal, romantic love, issues around self-worth, being controlled, or controlling others. What you don't generally decide is exactly how you are going to experience these lessons.

"Let us say that you are working on self-worth issues, and your basic premise is that you cannot accomplish anything because you are poor and stupid. You can continue to replay those identities for the entire lifetime, or you can start to find ways to change your impression of yourself.

"The predestination crowd would say you planned to be dumb and poor. However, you might read a book on affirmations and begin to tell yourself you are brilliant, and that your brilliance will enable you to become rich. You start to excel at school, get a fellowship to do research, get national recognition, and win monetary prize after prize. You have manifested a realization about your self-worth by using your abilities to become recognized as brilliant and, in consequence, wealthy.

"If you follow only your thoughts, you make it impossible to change your feelings about yourself. These thoughts are a combination of dreams, expectations, and what you have absorbed from seeing, hearing, and reading what *other* people think. You may imagine that these thoughts (although not really yours) are pre-ordained and nothing you say or do will change them.

"You acknowledge that your confusion arises from whether to exercise freedom of choice by seizing your own power, or sit back and accept what others plan for you—but you are the master of your soul. You alone are the driver of each lifetime. You alone determine the pathway, whether by manifesting what you would like to experience, or by sitting back and taking whatever comes."

Making contracts

Some people have a very romantic view of the expression "soul mate." They think we have just one Mr. Right or Ms. Right with whom to fall in love, marry, and live happily ever after. The reality is none of this. First, we were broken off from Source in a batch of souls usually numbering 144. Out of this big group we choose to work with a small number of soul mates; from our core group of 12 to 18, there are, at most, 6 to 8 souls with whom we regularly incarnate at the same time. Second, while one of our soul mates may choose to be our life partner, the relationship may well be distressful to us because our two souls chose conflict or abuse to be the hallmark of that relationship. Third, happy relationships are often found outside our group of soul mates. Remember, our purpose in being here is to experience negativity. We often use our soul mates to give us the *negative* experiences we choose to have as life lessons.

The Masters wrote: "You made arrangements with some of your [soul mates] to help you experience various challenges. You may have wished to feel what betrayal, abandonment, upheaval, or a sense of loss is like. You didn't always determine the exact manner in which the lessons would be played out, but just the end result. Betrayal may be a broken promise to a child, a cheating husband, or false accusations from a close colleague. Abandonment may be when your partner or parent walks out on you, or the death of a close family member or friend.

"Being in the midst of a devastating natural event, or being uprooted as a child by your parents to move to another location, may be your expression of upheaval. You can experience a sense of loss from the death of a parent, child, or pet, or in the loss of your employment. Each of these examples affords you the desired lesson."

Conflicts and the soul

"On a soul level we do not judge things to be 'good' or 'bad.' That does not mean that your soul while incarnate on the planet cannot sense the energy of society in judging things that way. But it also means that a soul has the choice *not* to get involved in things outside its lesson plan.

"The soul cannot have the full human experience unless it has an aspect of self that is ego-based. If the soul remained completely bathed in unconditional love it could experience nothing new. Some of the lessons that a soul chooses to learn deal with an interaction in the physical and emotional traumas impacting people around them. However, many soul lessons involve only the soul's personal interactions with those around them.

"The soul lesson may involve a larger group of players, who have chosen, for example, to become involved in an earthquake or in a war. This may lead the individual soul to allow the circumstances of the event to dictate how its human life will be subjected to the group activity. For instance, the souls involved on both sides of Hitler's rise to power were caught up in the events with their own prior permission. However, in situations of this kind, some souls become so involved in this fashion that they do not face the challenges they came to Earth to complete.

"Remember, each soul makes its own choices. One soul cannot make choices for another. To get entwined in a conflict, speak out about it, or protest the actions of a group may be part of a lesson in self-worth, or a recognition of your own power, or a refusal to be controlled by another, or even the experience of getting sucked up in a group hysteria.

"Whatever the true reason for a soul's activity, the worth may be evaluated by going inside and asking, 'Why am I doing this? What do I seek to gain myself out of this action?' If the answer has to do with a lesson or emotion you are trying to understand, it is part of your journey. If the answer is to 'show' those people, examine your motives because you are mirroring something you need to face about yourself."

Identifying life lessons

"You already have signposts in your life that say: "This is a life lesson." Never seen them? Of course you have, but you have just not recognized them. Any time you have a *fear* in life, or a *doubt* about what action you should take, you are looking face to face at a lesson. Just take your time and work through each task.

"When you become aware of them, stop for a moment and ask: Where does this come from? How do I feel about this fear? Does it relate to some other experience I have had and avoided? Do I think of something that seems totally unrelated, like a statement about my abilities from the past? Delve deeply into the feelings surrounding each fear and doubt—those are the outlines of your learning session.

"All the fears and doubts belong to you; you have plenty of things to do for yourself—no chance to get confused with someone else's lessons. Nothing is too harsh

168

for you, because you never set out to be confronted with more than you are able to handle in a lifetime. Take and clear each concern as it arises. It is not necessary to identify the lessons by definition, such as: this one is about abuse, that one about ego. When you reach a state of being at peace with your life, no longer facing doubts and fears, you have completed this life's desired work. Then playtime may commence!"

Whatever comes your way

"We frequently hear the question: 'How are we supposed to know what life lessons we are here to learn?' We hear it from young and old, all nationalities, all practicing religious beliefs, and just about everyone in human form. Well, fasten your seat belts because we have the answer:

Whatever comes your way is what you need to experience.

"What you need to experience is what you planned to learn before you came down to Earth. You selected all the categories of lessons you wanted to have, once you were in body form, and so you set up the sequences of events that would precipitate them. When you arrived on Earth you had amnesia so that you could face the lesson without previous knowledge and, in working through the lesson and understanding it, grow in wisdom, which was your ultimate goal.

"The reason this question appears so frequently is that humans need reassurance that they are right. The soul doesn't judge things as right or wrong. The soul wishes to experience things so that it may gain wisdom through evaluating whether the action is something it wishes to repeat, or whether it has learned enough to move on.

"Your human need for constant validation gives your power to 'those who know' so that you can be sure you are 'right.' What hogwash! Honor yourself! Take responsibility for your life, and work through what is in front of you so that you can move forward. Go inside and follow those feelings that tell you the direction you intended to take."

Completing life lessons

"Is it possible to complete all possible life lessons a soul may choose to experience in their Earthly incarnations in one lifetime? The answer is: not unless they could live the equivalent of hundreds of lifetimes in one body. The other way to look at the issue is: Is it possible for a soul to complete all the life lessons they chose for their lifetime, the average single span of a body, within that one lifetime? The answer is a resounding Yes!

"To gain all the possible knowledge of negativity possible on Earth, you must have experiences available only when present in each of the body's possible sexes. Limiting events generally require physical or mental inadequacies, while manipulation requires above-average intelligence, and physical experiences require a whole body.

"Enlightenment comes when the conscious mind becomes aware of the unconscious non-physical aspects of the soul. To speed up the process within a life, rid yourself of doubts and fears; turn from the ego judgment of the physical dimension to the evaluation love of all souls of the non-physical spiritual dimension. Tune into the universe and enter the energetic flow. Give up control, the need to know, and expectations. Have faith and trust in your feelings, not your mind. In other words, get to know the true essence of your unconditional loving soul while still incarnate!"

Why do we have life lessons?

The issue of life lessons is a tough one. It is easy to lose sight of the reason why we have them, and why they can be so difficult. Here are the Masters again:

"We wish to discuss with you something we hear from your planet so often: 'Why did I choose to come and experience this horrible life lesson?' This is frequently accompanied by despair and a sense of hopelessness.

"When the soul is at Home in its purest form, it resides in total unconditional love just like the Source from which it broke off. In order to appreciate the magnificence of self, the soul may choose to come down to planet Earth into a duality where every emotion and experience has an exact opposite. Exposure to that which is the opposite of unconditional love can awaken an appreciation of what has been lost.

"Before entering into a human shell and coming to Earth to live out a lesson, you observe all the possible things that are less than perfect. Without trying each one, though, it is just like reading something in a book but never having firsthand experience of it.

"For instance, marathons fascinate you; you can read all about them and watch them, yet never take part. Do you know what it is like to run a marathon? No! Until you have done the training, run the miles, and felt the exertion and exhaustion, it is merely a concept. Train for and run a marathon, and you gain the wisdom of the experience.

"Human life is the only way for your soul to gain the wisdom of the knowledge that has come to you. Experience the occurrence so that you may evaluate it to know whether you want to experience it again. That is a life lesson."

How you love yourself

"Spiritual love is easily acknowledged in your life when you totally accept yourself exactly as you are at the moment. Does that sound a bit strange? To accept that you should love a body grossly overweight such that it is creating medical problems? What about accepting an addiction numbing you to your surroundings and separating you from the rest of the populace? Yes, we mean to accept all that is you! That is self-love. Self-love is unconditional love mirroring the Source energy of the universe. To not love the problem is to deny either that it exists or that you can learn enough to get rid of it from your life.

"Self-love is relishing the reason you have chosen to come into human form. That, simply, is to acknowledge, bring to your awareness, your life lessons. It is only when you can step away from fighting what you are here to confront that you can begin the journey that gives you the knowledge and wisdom required by your soul.

"Self-love is to accept—but definitely not to 'like'—the result or outward appearance of the lessons. This dislike becomes your motivation. You love that you have the strength to learn all about your lesson so you may reverse its deleterious effects upon your body. The love allows you to withdraw from the drama of the disliked task so you may dispassionately learn about it and find a solution to balance out the energy.

"When you love yourself your lessons pop into awareness as difficulties in life—things you don't like, but for which, by jumping in and rummaging around, you may find the cause and, with that, a solution. It may seem elusive, but it is really right there in your face! As your 'dislikes' lessen, your self-love thrives."

Should we just sit back and do nothing?

"There are all different kinds of lessons that a soul may choose to experience on Earth. Yes, Earth is the only planet that has a dual energy setup, with both negative and positive conditions. Our lessons appear as negative energies and it is for souls to determine how to deal with those situations and make them into positive experiences to learn about themselves and their issues—if they can.

"The question would seem to imply that even a soul who chooses to be a doctor is interfering with the patient's life lessons. But life is much more complicated than that. The doctor cannot go out and drag in patients off the street and force them to receive medical treatment. All healing has to do not only with the actions of the healer, but with the intentions of the patient as well. If people do not want to be healed they will find a way to remain out of balance or at dis-ease with their body. Part of their lesson may be to acknowledge that they need the help of another. So, if people realize why they are suffering from a condition, they can go and seek out a healer who can assist in remedying the state.

"In another example, good Samaritans might go to countries and help bring clean water to the people. After they leave, the inhabitants must maintain the water system; their lesson may be to take care of themselves.

"Only in a situation where people are trying to force their beliefs and lifestyle on others can there be a case of interference. But don't forget freedom of choice—the recipients can always ignore the offered help. In a case where souls may be diverted away from their lesson by the assistance of others, they will have the ability to try again to learn the lesson in that same lifetime or another.

"What do you do once the event is completed? That's the other side of the question. These experiences are called life lessons because you came to Earth to learn from them. In each of these scenarios, if you fight the emotions and feelings that come during the experience, you do not allow yourself to learn.

"You must embrace the energy of the experience so that you have an imprint of its power—then you will not need any further examples of that lesson. If you do not embrace the sensation, you do not make a record of the feeling, and so you must go through the experience again until you allow yourself to feel."

II. Life Lessons in Individual Experience

Our essays on abortion, healing, heaven, hell, homosexuality, and suicide deal with people's issues of concern in our study of the ideas coming from Home on the Other Side. Nothing is more central to our quest, however, than the question of the purpose of human life itself, and the nature of the lessons that we have chosen to learn while we are here on planet Earth. Understanding these things is crucial to our grasp of what life lessons are for and how they impact us. This makes for a significant difference in the way we will tackle the journey of our soul. The Masters' *Handbook* makes it seem simple: "Souls leave Home for planet Earth in order to experience lessons there. They return Home to appreciate, understand, and affirm the wisdom their journeys have afforded them."

Now for some case studies:

Mahatma Gandhi

Why do we need to learn lessons in the first place? Is not our celestial Home a place of absolute perfection, of unconditional love? A good basic explanation was given to us in our interview of Mahatma Gandhi's soul:

"The purpose of human life is to learn as much as we can about ourselves and to learn lessons. At Home we're in an ocean, an all-consuming environment of unconditional love. Here we do not feel hate, despair, or any emotions or feelings that would be considered negative. It is only by assuming a human body that we are able to experience these things, yet in each one of the seemingly negative experiences of our lessons, our appreciation and wisdom concerning the unconditional love from which we come grows, magnifies, and intensifies. So we come to Earth to partake of the lessons we may learn there in order that we may grow in appreciation of what we have at Home and who we are as a soul, a piece of the all-encompassing divinity [of Source]. Unconditional love has no sensation to it. It is a state of being in which everything is perfect. In order to understand what everything perfect is like, you must know what less-than-perfect is."

Martin Luther King

The soul of Martin Luther King, Jr. continued this process of enlightenment:

"To understand this whole thing, you have to appreciate that the sense of right or wrong is a judgment issue, and that judgment exists only in physical form. When we are at Home with our advisors, we decide what lessons we want to experience. The purpose of a lesson is to gain wisdom—what it feels like, how it enriches, how it enlightens, how it contributes to the growth of who we are as an essence.

"When people decide to experience negativity, they can experience it in minor ways, such as not being in control of themselves, always being directed by others as to what to do, always being told in Earth terms that what they're doing is wrong, which crushes their self-worth. Or they can be instigators of negativity, such as the role chosen by Hitler, in which he took a form to cause people immense suffering and physical stress.

"Once we decide what we want to do, we go down and experience it. Again, this is a lesson, so it may take us an entire lifetime, or more than one lifetime, to get to the point where we truly understand that lesson, where we can assume the wisdom of knowing what effect it has upon a human soul, how energetically it affects our essence. That point can come during our first lifetime experiencing it, or we can go through several lifetimes, learning pieces of it during each, and all of a sudden in one lifetime it clicks. The lights come on; we understand; we feel; we know; we become as part of the wisdom that we were seeking. Once that point is reached, we have the choice to continue to bask in the energy that we have come around to, or we may decide to change direction because we have the wisdom we sought.

"We don't come down with a detailed plan: 'I am going to understand what negativity is, and I'm going to do it exactly this way.' We never have 'exacts,' and the reason we don't establish an exact formula is that if we do that beforehand, we are restricted by what we can experience, and if any of the other participants change the parameters, we aren't flexible enough to be able to take that change as an enrichment of the lesson we're learning. We just ignore it and miss out on the opportunity to be enriched, and therefore we might have to come back and do the lesson again because we didn't explore all of the possibilities.

"To sum it all up, we decide what lessons we want to learn. We don't decide all of the facets of how we're going to learn those lessons. It is once we get here in physical form that we say, 'Oh, that didn't quite give me the sense of what that emotion is; let me try this other way to sense it, to feel it, and see if it resonates more with me.' So we have the freedom of choice of how we experience our lessons, and we don't decide that until we're here in physical form. The predetermination is the base outline of the lesson. The freedom of choice is how we choose to do it, which is constantly evolving while we are in physical form."

You may be feeling that this explanation was going a little too fast. Let us break these statements down a little.

Our essence, as fragments of Source, is unconditional love, and we dwell at Home in an atmosphere of unconditional love. This is perfection and perfect creativity. But we need, as it were, a mirror to understand who we are. We need darkness for us to understand what light is like. We need to experience the negative in order to grasp what the positive is truly like. So we come to Earth's controlled atmosphere specifically to experience negativity in all its forms. Doing so helps us to understand our self.

Jesse Owens

The Olympic runner Jesse Owens had this straightforward explanation of his experiences:

"My life purpose was to be put into a situation where I had to deal with adversity—financial hardship, skin color, weakness of body and having to build it up—and in all of this to find that the important thing is the heart and soul inside. That is where the energy is. "

The *Handbook* adds a further explanation:

"While at Home, the soul and Source are composed of amorphous energy which swirls around, comingling and sharing in the beautiful energy in which all exist. In order to feel any negativity or lessening of that fantastic energy, a soul must have a physical body. *A body provides the nerves and emotions for the sensation of negativity or loss to be felt.*"

The Masters explain that in order to provide a controlled environment in which souls might effectively experience both positive and negative lessons, planet Earth was programmed to have a balance between the two. This they call the "duality" of Earth, and one may imagine that statue of a lady (Justice) holding a pair of scales, with the positive on one side perfectly balanced by the negative on the other.

Frank Sinatra

Frank Sinatra's soul had a broad experience of both aspects of duality in his human life:

"I had pre-planned to examine all of the strata of human existence, from the poorest of the poor to the rich and privileged; from the meek, mild, church-going life to the raucous outlaw. I wanted a touch of everything, a taste of everything. I had set out to have a smorgasbord. I accomplished each of the goals I had set for myself by my free choice. Sometimes I chose to immerse myself in an aspect of life, and sometimes I stayed on the outskirts—just observing friends, relatives, and others who were within the whirlpool while I remained on solid ground."

Elvis Presley

Elvis Presley now also sees aspects of his life as having an essentially positive direction:

"One of the lessons I wanted to learn was that of being able to build myself, within the framework of humankind, to be able to determine who I was, and to go from rags to riches, as you say on Earth."

Walt Disney

Walt Disney had difficulties to overcome, but felt that he had succeeded:

"My biggest lesson was that if you had faith in yourself, you could accomplish anything you sought to accomplish, so that regardless of whatever obstacles were placed in your way, either by your family or by society in general, faith and trust in yourself would allow you to do what you wanted to do. I did accomplish that. I did take the noose that at some point I felt was around my neck because of my father's and grandfather's failures."

Mother Teresa

Mother Teresa had wanted to share her strong inner drive for self-understanding with other people:

"Part of my life lesson was to find myself. My journey was to use my humanness to help others find what they needed, a sense of worth in themselves, a way to sustain themselves. It was not the food that I provided for them; it was not the medicine that I enabled them to receive. It was, if they could go within themselves, a sense of who they were inside. Of course, I tried to give this to them on an unconscious level because it was part of my own soul's journey."

Yehudi Menuhin

Classical musician Yehudi Menuhin came to Earth to accomplish two things; one was positive, the other turned out to be negative, in the form of ill health:

"As I was planning to come down...there were certain things I wished to accomplish in the form of communication with music. Those were the lessons I came down with. The secondary lesson was dealing with the medical problems I had, and doing it in such a way that it did not define who I was—that, as a matter of fact, it was very much unknown by so many people, because to me it wasn't important. It was the sign that if I dealt with that, that was the last of the big lessons I had to accomplish while in physical form. My life's purpose, then, became to instill in others the joy and the love and the importance of musical communication. The way for me to do that was with the various programs that I became involved in, so it was my life's purpose that continued; I was one of the fortunate souls who had about a fifty-fifty life: 50% of lessons and 50% of life purpose. "

III. Preparation For Life Lessons

It is at Home that we make the decision to come to Earth and learn lessons. We have help, but the choices of lessons, when they are made, are wholly and freely ours. Lessons we choose involve decisions about gender, parentage, personal gifts, and whether our lessons should be to receive negative experiences or to become agents of negativity ourselves. Let's take these things in order. First we consider our Council of Advisors. Each soul has a council of 12 advisors, drawn from our group of soul mates:

Wilma Rudolph

"We all have a council of twelve that helps us decide what we want to do when we incarnate. But even in spirit form we have freedom of choice, so while we get advice and suggestions from our council, it is solely up to us to decide exactly what we want to do. In [my] particular case, a lot of the ideas came from me because I was building up to that sort of lifetime. I had many dry runs, or previews in different lifetimes, of being a leader, being a guide, being able to overcome obstacles. This life as Wilma Rudolph was designed to put all the pieces together into one gigantic, dynamic example of the power and strength of the soul within a body.

Marilyn Monroe

"[We have] total freedom. We have a council of advisors who are always sitting down with us, and we are saying, you know, I've experienced this and this. I haven't done that and that. Do I want to try that? Well, I don't know. We go back and forth until we come up with a plan. Then, once we have a plan, we start finding the best ways to implement it. But it's all about things we wish to learn and experience."

Jesse Owens

"Each soul, before coming into a body, meets with advisors, sometimes called a council of twelve (at times it's not the whole group but just the main guides who are going to help you in that particular lifetime). You take a look and ask what it is you want to experience in that lifetime. For instance, to compare this life with my Roman life: In that lifetime I was lauded and given everything I needed and treated like a prince, and this life was to see if I could create the same results with the exactly opposite 'building materials,' so to speak. The decisions were solely mine. The possible scenarios were contributed by some of my advisors."

The choices of country, tribe, class, family, parents, and the soul's own gender are all freely made by the soul before incarnating. The Masters add, "The soul asks itself if gender is a major or minor aspect of its human life. Decisions are made accordingly."

Sylvia Plath

"Did you choose before incarnating to experience clinical depression?"

"That was one of the lessons I wished to experience in human form. I wanted to know what it was to have a sense of foreboding overriding my entire existence and have a cloud over me that I had to find my way in."

"What would the benefit of such a choice be for you?"

"To enjoy the sunshine, to enjoy a sense of freedom, and a sense of being able to see and connect with everything that was out there. Unless you experience the opposite of something, you can't truly appreciate what the ultimate experience can be."

Louis Armstrong

"Did you deliberately choose to have a father who would walk out on your mother?"

"Yes. I needed to be able to find myself at an early age. I needed to find out how I could affect other people, and it was what I was going toward with making that choice."

James Baldwin

"We always choose where we're coming to and it can be for a number of reasons. It can be for the turmoil expected within the family. It can be because of the genetics that are running through a particular family line so that we will experience disabilities, diseases, addiction tendencies— things of that nature, or because we have contracts with some of the parties who are also going to be in that family."

Andy Warhol

The issue of sexual orientation, as we saw earlier, usually follows a broader choice:

"I chose to experience ambivalence, which was the period of time before I accepted and told others that I was in fact homosexual. It was a constant battle of: Am I doing this to be different? Am I doing this because I'm actually being accepted by a male partner rather than a female partner? Or am I doing it because that is what my body and my mind need at this time? I did put all of those patterns together for something I wished to experience in this lifetime."

Albert Einstein

The choice of genius is a special decision made in advance of incarnation:

"I had chosen to experience what it was like to be totally wrapped up in my studies, in my ways of converting the workings of the universe into an account that was palatable to human beings. I also came down with my ideas and writings, to be able to spark other people to develop an entire cache of information that would enrich the planet.

"[Genius] is prearranged, because a person creates the lessons they wish to experience. If it were possible for a person to come down in a normal body and then develop into a genius, they would not be able to fulfill the normal lessons they came down to learn—such as hate, love, abuse, abandonment. They would be totally overshadowed by the form of genius. The effect that genius has upon a person is to isolate them, so geniuses, in order to be able to sustain themselves, have to possess a foreknowledge of what they are doing, even though it is unconscious. In this way they do not find that the loneliness of converting ideas for human knowledge and understanding detracts from their existence.

That person who is a successful genius needs to have a good contact within themselves to their soul, to feel that connection, and to feel the love from within their soul that is for themselves. In this way they do not lapse into some kind of self-destructive behavior because they are not loved or accepted by anyone, or because they are not able to interact with anyone."

The Masters add: "The soul will also ask if it has any skills developed in prior lives that will not interfere with its learning but will help with some other things in this new life. A soul might bring its music, its communication skills, or even its psychic abilities into play."

Marian Anderson

"While we are in spirit form we decide what lessons we wish to take and what our spiritual purpose, our pathway, will be. I had decided that, first, I would be in a situation where I had to learn my worth and to claw myself out of oppression. Then, with my physical tools, I would be able to lift people out of the emotionally binding places from whence I had learned to release myself. A number of my prior lives had been musical, so I already had a feeling within my soul of the vibration of music. That's why from an early age the vibration of music was my entire life."

IV. Soul Contracts

How does the soul make sure that it receives the life lessons it is looking for, when it incarnates? The best way is to create a contract with another soul mate whom we trust, for this to be provided. Let us take the illustration of a situation where one soul, who has chosen to be female, wishes to experience sexual abuse. Its soul mate, who intends to be a male, has already had that experience in a previous life, and this time wishes to play the role of a sexual abuser. This is effected by the two souls' acting out their chosen roles in each other's life. This scenario may be one of several similar contracts each soul has made for that lifetime.

Carmen Miranda

"There was a feeling of affinity toward certain souls, who I now know were, in fact, soul mates of mine. Interactive soul mates are those who are most important to us during each physical lifetime, those with whom we make contracts for the lessons we wish to experience. They provide for us circumstances that on Earth may be considered negative, and they provide positive influences for us as well."

Anne Frank

"Soul groups are energies, which you call souls, who split off from the Source about the same time. When we prepare to go into human form we make our most serious contracts with soul mates to learn the most in-depth lessons. They have shared so many lives with us that we can depend upon them, and they know us well enough, and we know them well enough that we are confident they will do a good job of helping us learn our lessons.

"Some lessons are considered 'good' lessons, such as being a loving spouse (if we are going to examine the lesson of being in physical love and having a family). Others are considered 'bad' lessons, such as when you want to experience degradation and depravation, with your soul mate possibly being a slave master over you."

Eleanor Roosevelt

"We do not plan during our between-lives what effect we are going to have on other people (unless it is a person with whom we have entered into a contract). We are only concerned, when we are on the planet, with what an experience will mean to us as an individual. One of my big lessons...was to feel abandonment. It was what put me into self-reflection, first in the imaginary world, and then grasping what was reality. This grew into my drive to change what the world actually was into something much more palatable to me: a place where there was more a sense of equality and where those less fortunate were afforded respect."

Babe Ruth

In this instance the contract centered on a schoolmaster's physical punishment of the rebellious youthful Babe Ruth:

"One of my life lessons was discipline, so I was put into a place where I would be able to examine what discipline was. Of course, as my life at that time showed, I had no discipline. I had no one to tell me what was right and wrong, so I made my own rules. I was left to my own devices and became totally incorrigible, and so rather than wreck all that my parents had built so carefully, I was shipped off [to school]. This was the idea within my life: to know what it was to have no limits, then to be in a situation where everything was limited."

"Did Brother Matthias have a contract with you as a soul to give you that discipline?"

"Absolutely. He's actually a soul mate of mine—a soul mate being someone who has the most impact on you, and with whom you make a contract—and he was the one who was there to put my feet to the fire, to say, 'This is what you wanted to deal with. You wanted to deal with discipline issues; here is how you can do it. Make the choice of whether you're going to learn this lesson or have to come back and do it again.'"

Selena Quintanilla Perez

"[Yolanda, who killed me,] had a path, just as I had a path. We had agreed, before coming down into physical form, that my life would end with her, and that she would have the experience of incarceration and restriction of freedom, as she is still having. As a matter of fact, she and I have had a number of lives together. We're soul mates. As with practicing something that is very noteworthy within a human life, so you make an agreement with somebody whom you can trust or with whom you've made other agreements, who you know will be able to carry it through."

V. Human Ethics and Soul Choices

We have seen, in a general way, that souls do not come down to Earth to bask in the sunshine of a good, untroubled life. In Earth's duality, negative experiences co-exist with positive ones. We learn about our inner nature (the positive essence of who we are) by holding up the mirror of negative experience to ourselves. But we are not forced to do so. We incarnate having made choices of the lessons we want to learn, though not of the circumstances by which we will be confronted with them.

Having the need to experience negativity from the inside means that we cannot say that if we take on a negative role we are "bad," any more than the talented actor who plays the villain in a play is "bad." We are very like actors on the stage of planet Earth.

Quotations from our interviews round out this picture:

Bertrand Russell

"What matters in the soul's perspective is the richness of the experience of the lessons it learned while in physical form. In physical form, what matters is that you experience lessons, whether they are humanly considered to be good or evil, so you can take that energy back to add to the richness of the experiences of all the souls."

Judy Garland

"My purpose was to experience the struggle, the depths of depression which would come if you were totally run as a puppet by an outside force. I always felt there was a string of puppeteers marching me through life experiences, not allowing me to make any decision, not allowing me to choose any particular direction. The only thing that I could choose to do was to numb myself to the experience. As souls we can view a movie but we cannot be an actor in the movie. We have to assume a physicality [put on a body] in order to do that. Once we are in physical form and actually take part in a movie, we can then experience, and know, and gain the wisdom of what it takes to play each one of those particular parts, rather than just see someone acting and assume what it feels like to experience what the actors are experiencing."

William James

"Hitler came down to Earth to experience a number of things, including extremes of hatred, and to experience going from the situation of being belittled and misunderstood [in his youth] to that of becoming a dominating dictator. These were all lessons he came to learn. His intention within the lessons was to do the best in each situation that he could. When he was in the realm of pure hatred his intent was to hate everything, so in that example it was intent that caused consequences. He also had the unenviable position, for humans, of being a teacher of many people around him.

"If anyone has the intent to learn a lesson to the best of their ability, it is no different if they are a Hitler or a healer—if it is done with the intent of learning....Ethics are an invention of those in human form. Ethics do not exist with us at Home because we are in unconditional love. We do not have to dictate or live by a set of standards that will make us be what we would like all people to be. Ethics are a construct to have all of the actions within a group of people be *fair* to each other. Each individual soul is in a body to experience certain lessons. Some of those lessons would be considered ethical by all who are around them, because they do not impact them in a negative way. Other lessons would be considered unethical because the person is wishing to learn the lesson of stretching the boundaries of what is then recognized by society. I now know neither is right nor wrong, and we cannot dictate to a soul to be 'ethical,' as we understand it, if they have a lesson to learn that is 'unethical.'"

Sharon Tate

"[Souls who take on negative roles] do it quite deliberately, and the reason is in order to experience it themselves and to give other souls the experience of knowing what it's like. One example is the demolition of the World Trade Center. Those perpetrators within the airplanes had agreed to be evil incarnate in the eyes of the world, again under the guise of some fanatical idea of what was right. All the souls who

189

transitioned [died] at that time had agreed to be on the stage, to communicate emotionally with everyone else on the planet, in order to change perspective, and to help them see that the world was tipping in the direction of anarchy."

Adolf Hitler

The ultimate test for many people is what we can say about ruthless dictators, such as Stalin, Pol Pot, or Hitler. This excerpt is from our interview with Hitler's soul:

"I saw the person whose part I was playing at that time as being what a human would consider as 'absolute evil.' But I am no different from any other soul who plays a part in order to learn physical lessons and to help others with their lessons. I was selected and agreed with others to be evil incarnate on the planet during the time I was Adolf Hitler.

"I was in that lifetime psychotic, although I would not have admitted it in that persona. I did play the psychotic. Who but a psychotic would be so ruthless, so unthinking, uncaring, uncompassionate, and diabolically cruel."

"What does the Creator achieve by permitting evil?"

"To be able to experience and know the greatness of what we are. We cannot truly comprehend unconditional love unless we know what the absence of unconditional love is like."

"Many will want me to ask if you are sorry for what you did."

"No, because I did what I agreed to do to those who chose to be victims. In doing that, there was a waveform created which allowed all souls to experience the ultimate in evil. I did not do evil from a soul's purpose to be evil. I did evil for a perception and for a template of evil, so people would know they did not have to experience that again."

Winston Churchill

Sometimes in its planning with the council, a group situation occurs on Earth of which the individual soul may take advantage. Winston Churchill paints the broader picture of how our involvement in times of war and persecution may be for our spiritual advantage:

"Here at Home we look upon achievement as learning lessons. If a soul has never been in a situation which takes personal sacrifice in order to develop, evolve, or work through its innermost desires, then the battlefield, the martyrdom, the persecution are still needed for it to experience those things. It is not a requirement for humanity that there be wars at this time; it is just that individual souls wish to experience those things. We cannot learn lessons for other people. The sacrifices we made should be a guideline for others so as not to repeat what we went through."

Eleanor Roosevelt

Because each soul has freedom of choice regarding the lessons it wants to learn, there is no control exercised on what sort of life it will have:

"If a person's soul is incarnated at a time of chaos, it is because it needs to experience that chaos. We cannot say that any time is right for one thing more than for another. I can only have feelings about my experiences while in human form, and the knowledge that people must be enabled to do their life lessons.

"As a whole, here in spirit form we do not plan for trends within society. We do not plan, for instance, that we will only have people incarnate who are not going to be in need of self-medication, so that there won't be any social chaos. We can only say that there are people who need to experience addiction, so they go through all of the associated problems, learn their lessons, then renew their strength, so that they can move on. If addicts all choose to incarnate at the same time, then we do have a problem with society, but it is no different from a time when those who choose to be dictators and power-hungry people are on the planet all at the same time, and you have wars."

VI. Experience and Wisdom

The Masters say, "At Home, Source and all souls possess the knowledge of what every soul has ever experienced. They do not, however, have the wisdom of the experience unless they have performed, lived through, or been a part of the experience itself. Here comes the limiting factor: for a soul to truly have the full wisdom of a situation it must understand why each party did what it did. This can only be done when the soul reaches inside the body and evaluates the experience with its heart and essence. This is the central experience of the Earth lesson journey."

Charles Darwin

"[Once souls arrive back Home], there is a period of debriefing, as the military say, to find out what lessons have been learned. Sometimes it is at this debriefing that a soul who has not understood, while in human form, the lesson that they learned on the planet, gets the 'Aha!' moment, when they realize why they experienced what they had experienced. And if it is truly felt, they can then go back and feel it again very quickly, or not even have to do it at all, because they go from just having the knowledge of the experience to having the wisdom that goes with that experience.

"The final goal is to exist in unconditional love at all times with the wisdom of all of the experiences that can be had of what is not unconditional love, with all of the wisdom a physical manifestation can allow by way of interaction, rather than just a commingling. While there is humanity still in existence, that allows the mature soul also to act as guide, but to have a front-row seat in the greatest play that has ever been staged."

Judy Garland

"Why do you have to play these parts?"

"Because otherwise we would not have the wisdom, the feeling that the experience brings to us. Take sports— you can be an avid sports fan but you do not know the amount of practice, the degree of exertion that is needed to be a top-notch athlete, unless you do it yourself. Once you have the experience of the performance, then that is something which cannot be taken away from you, because you know what it takes to reach the level of the top athlete, to reach the level of being the best.

"I was playing the role of the victim though almost the entirety of my life. It was a victimization, but that was something I had wished to experience in all of its various facets; it was one of my intentions when I came down to Earth. The others were to recognize the worth within myself (which I struggled with during my ... physical existence), and to search beyond myself for any connection with what it was to be a soul (something, again, which I did not do very much)."

Babe Ruth

We may have experiences but don't all learn our lessons sufficiently to gain the deeper level of wisdom that is our objective. Babe Ruth was frank about that:

"While in physical form, I did not completely learn everything I had chosen to experience. As I went through the review, as I left my body and went back Home into the energetic, spiritual body, I saw what I had done and felt the true depth and meaning behind all the situations I had placed myself in, and all of the anxieties that I had caused other people. I realized how I could have modified my behavior to live as a normal person would live. In the end, I realized everything I had done, the lessons I had attempted to learn, how I had fulfilled the physical activity of learning those lessons, and then, once I was non-physical, I integrated the learning so I won't have to learn them again."

Joe Louis

The great boxer was successful in making his experiences his own wisdom:

"I had to try to overcome people trying to push me down as a black man, and I had to learn to bury the anger that was there—then at the end totally get rid of it. I felt a lot of injustice in my youth and in my early days about what was being done to me that was not humane. The lesson I had to learn was that I had to live with myself, and in living with myself, if I was comfortable with where I was; it did not make any difference what other people said. I wanted to reciprocate in love to people who treated me in all-which-ways. There are a lot of lessons that come out of boxing. For me the lesson was a sense of faith and conviction that I could do something I set out to do. It was a molding of self-image. For other people a lot of times it was anger—they had been so put down by society that they were going to teach their opponent that they were not to be messed with. That was where the anger came in boxing. I never was trying to prove that I was better than somebody else; I was just trying to prove to myself that I was better than I had been taught."

VII. No Judgment

The Masters remember our difficulty in understanding the ideas of human ethics and religious teaching of good and evil. "Once the soul leaves the body it enters a state of unconditional love, void of any judgment concerning its actions on Earth connected with the lessons it decided to experience in that life. There is nothing to be condemned or rewarded."

Frank Lloyd Wright

"From up here, I don't see [the murder of seven people] as wrongful; no one up here sees it as wrongful, because we don't judge. We evaluate if it was a lesson that enriched our knowledge of the human and soul experience, and yes, in that it was very successful. Although it contained what in human standards were a lot of disasters, to me it provided a lot of rich feelings, putting me onto paths that I needed to explore and understand."

Joe Louis

"Nothing is 'judgment' at Home. Everything is 'what did you learn from that lesson? What do you know you will never do again from the lessons you've learned?' Everything you experience in physical form adds to your overall knowledge and your wisdom of the whole human experience. Whether, when we're in physical form, we consider it a 'good' or 'bad' experience, it's still an experience. So in spirit form it's simply more the wisdom of what you would choose to repeat or choose never to repeat in another life, were you to come back in physical form. Any sport that is a contact sport has violence in it, or the result can be viewed as being violent, but it is something that is needed by the participants to prove something to themselves. We don't judge violence any more than we judge cruelty. It is just a life lesson."

VII. Adversity, Illness, and Death

We return to the issue of negative experiences. The Masters wrote:

"There are many types of negativity, or the absence of unconditional love. First come the strong emotions of the human psyche. The many possible mental and emotional incidents all provide separate life lessons. An incarnate soul may choose to experience anger, hatred, betrayal, worthlessness, self-negation. Other negative experiences may be physical, possibly including cancer, broken bones, and torture. For all of these to be perceived a physical body is absolutely necessary."

Death is an issue that they did not mention. Largely it is seen in positive terms back Home, as the beginning of a new stage in the journey of the soul.

Jane Addams

"We plan our lives before we come down here in terms of the major things we wish to experience (though not exactly how we will experience them), but still they are major issues or lessons. My desire was to be in a position where I had problems with my body and was confined and restricted. This could have been accomplished (as in fact it was) with my spinal difficulties, or it could have come through having polio, or it could have resulted from an accident. I did not determine the exact way it was going to happen to me, just the fact I was going to have some physical restrictions."

Georgia O'Keeffe

"[My failing eyesight] taught me to be more connected with energy, the same thing I began to realize was in my paintings....The macular degeneration was, at first, a cooling down period for me. It was a time for retrospection, when I went back and re-lived within my mind the paintings of my life. But it was still a time when I could convey things with energy; I still taught people who came to me. I was able to teach them the feel of color, and depth, and energy. This was easy for me because I was not distracted by wanting to jump in and change this little piece or that little piece within the pictures they were creating."

George Orwell

"Was tuberculosis planned?"

"The exact form of the ailment—no. It was planned that I would have some chronic, subsequently debilitating disease so that I would have to fight for strength among all of my fights for survival."

Rachel Carson

This is a situation where death was planned for a purpose:

"Halfway through writing Silent Spring, *you were diagnosed with cancer and died at 56. Why did you get cancer?"*

"It was part of my plan to go out with a bang, so to speak—the bang being that I would put myself out there as the sacrificial lamb, the person to be blamed for exposing this stuff, but without any way to totally discredit me and what I had said, because I wouldn't be around. I had not pre-planned the exact cause of my demise. The physical cause was that I had done many, many tests with the various chemicals and had exposure to the chemicals, which had an effect upon my body. "

Sharon Tate

"[My murder] was definitely planned. I was going to go through a violent death, which would bring attention to a way of life and to a whole pattern of brainwashing that was going on—not only in the Manson sect but throughout a lot of other quasi-religious and hippie groups at that time. The exact person or people who were going to be the perpetrators? It was sort of a loosely gathered contract. My soul knew it was going to be from the group of which Manson was a part. The exact people who did it—that was the freedom of choice within the group."

Carl Jung

There are no accidents in the way the universe operates:

"[What is the situation where] something falling into the road causes our death?"

"The time has come for us to transition. We happen to go down that particular road at the right time for the mountain to fall on us so that we can transition, but we haven't determined beforehand the exact means of the transition....There are no accidents. It is generally something that the soul has previously wanted to experience. If a woman is in an accident where she is maimed, it is because on the soul level, before coming into the body, she wished to experience what it was like to go through life with a handicap. Yet she was born whole so that she could know what it was like to be whole, then the event happens that makes her handicapped, so she gets the feeling of both sides.

"[Our souls choose tough lessons] because we gain wisdom. We learn by the suffering of others, and we get an emotional connection, even though we have not actually experienced it. The soul comes down and wants to have the wisdom of what a person feels it is like to suffer total deprivation, so that when they go back Home, the unconditional love here is so much sweeter, so much more immense."

IX. Summary

Life lessons are chosen by us, quite freely, in the planning stage before we incarnate on planet Earth. They represent our primary reason for existing outside of Source, the energy of which we all share. Lessons truly learned are not mere experiences; they hold up a mirror to us and show us who we are and our essence, which is unconditional love.

In order to be a such a mirror, our lessons will take us into uncharted waters. We will be assailed by all the negative experiences that flesh is heir to. That's the point of being on Earth. Without a human body—its nerves, its sensitivity to pain, and its stubborn, interfering ego—we would not have a clear picture. Nor would we have a broad range of experience unless we were also capable of being negative—perpetrators of what human ethics call "evil" as well as those who have evil done to them.

As actors in the great play of human existence we take roles to play. But they are only roles, showing us what we are not. So there is not judgment concerning the things we do on the world's stage. Experience, providing it is assimilated and becomes our inner wisdom, is just that— experience. And it is up to us to get to know the soul within our bodies for all its perfection, and not be trapped into seeing only the human half of the cosmic picture.

Human beings all live in a competitive, judgmental world where they are expected by others to perform this way or that, to believe this way or that, and to express themselves with ethical behavior that is "approved" as correct.

Not so the eternal soul, the essence of which is cooperative, not competitive; it is remarkably disinterested in the world's ethical and judgmental standards and correct behavior. The soul does not need to be told how to behave; it is totally loving. The parts it plays are in the role of an actor in Earth's little drama. It is free to be a saint or a sinner, the abused wife or her abuser, the thief or the victim. What the soul seeks to discover is the magnificence of its own nature by looking in the mirror of life, a life that contains enough negativity, by way of life lessons, to show the contrast.

It takes a while, sometimes many lifetimes, to work it all out, but when the task is completed a relationship is forged between the human ego and the eternal soul. At last the individual understands, even as it is also perfectly understood.

~ * ~

Life on the Other Side

(We ask the Masters questions)

The celestial Home

Masters, humans call the dimension where you live by a variety of words such as "Home," and "The Other Side." We would like to ask you which of the following descriptions is truly indicative of the location where souls reside when they are not incarnate on planet Earth or elsewhere:

First: Home?

"We have frequently referred to the non-physical state as "returning Home." We do that partially to convey the feelings most have about the comfort and security of their home. We also use the term to portray a point of origin, or the sayings: "Home is the place they always have to take you in," or "Home is where the heart is." [laughter] That has nothing to do with a soul, but to the human mind it feels good. Home is a term that also is used to indicate the beginning and the end, as in your American baseball's home plate."

Second: The Other Side?

"The Other Side" refers to the opposite of human or physical, as in "non-physical," since you do not have a container [body] restricting you any longer."

Third: The Fifth Dimension? What is a dimension—a vibration or a wavelength? And how many dimensions are there?

"Here again your language and practices determine the completeness of our answer for your satisfaction. In the messages we have delivered to you through this channel, we have talked in terms of three primary dimensions for simplification and classification.

"The third dimension is the physical dimension, ruled by the ego, where everything is judged. The head and the thinking mind determine what is right, and—oh, boy!—is there just one right and wrong!

"We talk then of discovering freedom of choice to make decisions on your own without input from society but rather from your heart, feelings, or intuition. This we call the fourth dimension. It is an in-between place from the completely physical and the completely non-physical fifth dimension.

"What we term the fifth dimension is residing in the non-physical state without connection to the physical realm.

"If you read some of the current New Age material you will find distinctions from some writers detailing minor differences between as many as 200 dimensions. That is making distinctions without a difference, like saying a color is green and then breaking it down into forest, sage, mint, Kelly, chartreuse, celery, lime, or just plain green. This is a case where we feel the distinctions get in the way of understanding. What is all that for, anyway? Again you humans are judging and grading experience.

"In the way we refer to dimensions, the physical aspects, as they relate to the human body, are perceived as dense for the third dimension, less dense when between dimensions in the fourth, and having no perception of a density at all when in the fifth—because the body ceases to be involved.

"We alternately use the term 'vibration' to indicate an imperceptible feeling of energy in the density of the third, which becomes more perceptible in the fourth, and finally gives a total sensation of all existing vibrations in the fifth. Vibration is a sensation of the movement of energy. Wavelengths are the way that humans can measure vibrations in the third dimension and sometimes beyond. How many of each exist? It depends how you want to grade and classify them."

Fourth: The Light? Is there really a physical light? How can it be seen if you have no eyes?

"Light implies a number of things. It stands for the comparison between what the human eye sees as brightness and darkness. Something that is light can be less dense or heavy. In the human judgment realm, positive things are called light and negative things are called dark. To reside in a positive, less dense, clear, and bright area you are said to be 'in the light.' One who strives to reach a negative-free existence and to help others also is called 'a light-worker.'

"For the person confused about the non-physical existence, when they have a near-death experience, meditate on crossing over, or dream about transitioning to that other state, they frequently see the junction between life and death as a tunnel of bright light. White light symbolizes purity, being without stain or baggage, leaving all the negativity behind. A very desirable place to be. When you are dreaming, in meditation, or under hypnosis, your optic nerves are not being stimulated, yet you 'see' without the use of your eyes."

Fifth: Heaven? I think we have already expressed in the book what you teach.

"Heaven is a term organized religion adopted to be the ultimate place of reward. Hell is the ultimate place of punishment. Either term contains a duality, an automatic opposite. Since the non-physical existence of Source (and

203

therefore all souls) is a place of unconditional love, void of any negativity, heaven and hell cannot exist as you have been taught. These states exist only on Earth. Of course it is possible for you to use the concept you envision as perfection, and apply the term 'Heaven,' 'Nirvana,' or even 'XYZ-scene' to it. After all, you are the ones who create the reality of your existence."

You have also indicated that souls live in "unconditional love" and that they are connected with the energy of Source, which is the same. Can you be explicit about this energy and love?

"It is very difficult to answer your questions in a way that comports with your language and understanding. It is akin to describing to someone who has never explored a cave what that experience is like: to be able to feel both the freedom and confinement of that situation, and at the same time, the sense of the mass above you, and the beauty of being a part of the planet—the fear and the excitement. All have to be lived in order to be appreciated.

"For an Earth comparison, unconditional love equates with bliss! Few achieve full unconditional love in a human body—the closest would probably be the love between mother and child. This state of bliss is difficult to achieve between a man and a woman because most set conditions upon the activities of the other, mostly in the realm of monogamy. But a parent, particularly a mother, sees her child as perfect. She also sees the child as an extension of herself and, therefore, always doing exactly what s/he should.

"We all are facets of the Source energy of the universe. By 'energy' we mean to convey a sense of a state of awareness of everything that exists. In the beginning we were a unity, and were all-powerful, all-knowing, all-creative; existence was perfection. But even perfection can be boring and yet not totally known or appreciated. We sought to examine how wonderful our perfect unconditional love was by experiencing what it was not. To do this we had to create a negative, or place of lacking of love. That was planet Earth.

How do souls maintain their connection with Source energy?

"Our fragments of Source, souls, left the unity to try out this negative energy and evaluate it in comparison to our true nature. While contained within a 'shell' [body] we appear to be separate from our unity but in fact are always connected. To the thinking mind within a physical body, those conscious connections of being a part of Source are blocked so that our past knowledge will not influence our current experiments. If we remember who we truly are, we remove the blockage and open the connection."

Is unconditional love at Home the same as the energy of Source throughout the universe, or are there differing levels of love energy?

"Outside of a restrictive body shell, energy is felt the same, regardless of the experiences we have gone through. There are no differing levels of unconditional love. The only thing that seems to influence what is perceived by the soul, is its own self-imposed filters—usually incomplete life lessons that it wants to continue working through. These are hangovers from the dense third-dimensional life on Earth."

You have indicated the Source energy is sentient. How is this expressed, as you also state the Source is energy, not a god-person?

"Sentience is a state of awareness of the things occurring around you and the ability to respond to them by way of memory that influences and sculpts its use. It is only the restrictions of the human mind that require sentience to be contained within a defined space or a human body. The idea that Source or Creator must be something similar to yourself is saying all things must be identical to whatever you previously experienced. Since you have not experienced a thinking, calculating, non-physical mass, you do not list it as a possibility. Source does not have a container or body; it is part of every particle in the universe, and every particle in every atom as a whole is Source."

Was one of the purposes of Source's breaking souls off from itself, and allowing each soul to have individuality, the way Source was able to create personality without compromising its distinct energy?

"No, again you are able to relate only to Earth experiences. We find it amusing that you use the term 'personality.' To have a personality you must have a person, and non-physical energy has no personality. Ego must be present to grade or judge personal qualities. A personality has a recognized set of characteristics associated with the manner in which a physical body responds to stimuli. You are talking about the human experience. Source sought to observe the negative aspects of the human experience, not to change its essence based upon what it observed, but merely to understand the magnificence of self. The role one plays does not change who that being is in fact."

The community of souls

How big is the universal community of souls?

"This question is a little like how many grains of sand are there upon the beach? Does it really make a difference? Would it make you feel less or more important? There are enough souls to populate Planet Earth, hundreds of other planets, all the souls currently having life reviews as they leave one form of existence for another, all the guardian souls who have never entered a physical state, and all those who are deciding what to do next. The number, as you record things on Earth, would be too large for you to comprehend."

How many souls are there currently in existence? Is the creation of new souls ongoing or has it already met a target number?

"Using your numbering system there are approaching a trillion souls in existence. Take your known Earth population, consider there are hundreds of other places souls can inhabit, understand souls come and go daily (birth and death), some souls are in places where they have the option of popping in and out of bodies as they experience different activities, and the answer is that the number changes constantly. The creation of individual souls has no specific target number. All the fragments that are needed to sustain the current learning processes exist now. Will more be needed in the future? There are too many variables to say with absolute certainty, but we do not anticipate the creation of any additional souls."

What proportion of all souls are currently incarnate on Earth? What proportion of the souls on Earth are currently discarnate?

"Less than ten percent of all the energetic pieces of Source, which we call souls, are incarnate on your planet Earth. This is not a static number but flows like the tides on the beach; it is ever changing. Discarnate souls are a very small fraction of those who choose a human existence. Less than one-tenth of one percent of the incarnate souls opt to stay in the in-between phase from human to free soul at Home. It is only those who are still committed to a life lesson and cannot let go."

Will souls ever fully return to merge within the energy of Source and thereby lose their individuality?

"Souls always remain a part of Source regardless where their focus is directed. Consider for the moment that Source has divided itself into various things in order to have a multitude of experiences. An easy way to understand might be for you to consider a beehive. A hive is a community with a single consciousness. Individual bees communicate with the rest of the hive to tell them what they have discovered. They go forth and gather materials necessary for the growth of the whole. When they return home they are just part of the mass; however, they have the specific memory of the particular flowers that they visited that no one else may have seen. They lose their individuality but not their experiences. Such is the relationship between the initial Source and its particles."

Is the duality of Earth going to change when Source is fully supplied with Earth-gathered wisdom?

"Is your question will Earth ever completely fulfill the reason it was created? The answer is no—not unless or until every soul who desires to experience negativity and freedom of choice has been able to do so. The population may vary, making it seem as if negative or positive energy is getting the upper hand, but that does not happen. You are just seeing a segment of the whole."

What other areas/dimensions/planets are important centers in the life of souls? How does Earth rank in terms of its strategic importance?

"A soul in its pure form is energy. Energy does not have the physical senses you are familiar with, which allow you to see, hear, smell, feel, and have emotional reactions. All of these things can be observed, and the knowledge of them conveyed from one soul to another, but the individual soul may yearn to experience the sensation itself.

"In order to feel the exertion necessary to swim the English Channel you must do it. To know what life is like in a wheel chair, dependant on other people, you must endure it. These things may be accomplished by going to Earth and setting them up as a life lesson, or by going to some other place specifically established to experience physical prowess and exhaustion, or total dependence without additional life factors such as dealing with family and growing up. These staged arenas are some of the other areas available for a soul to sample. None is of more or less importance, since we do not judge right and wrong. We merely evaluate an experience and see if we have learned what we set out to accomplish. Earth is the place to learn all about freedom of choice: nowhere else has that as a factor.

[Laughing] "The old ranking question! We don't rank; we just evaluate what we can learn from the various situations. None is more important than any other. As to location, they are all around you: in your galaxy and others, in your time dimension and others, in your vibration and others. Some souls choose to spend all their time in just one type of experience, such as repeated trips to Earth and nowhere else. Others shop around to sample what's available."

Is the humanoid body form replicated elsewhere in the universe?

"There are approximations of the human body on other planets that have a similar atmosphere. There are generally changes to accommodate the difference on their surface. Does the species want to have to consume solid physical food for maintenance, or are they satisfied with breathing in the nourishment needed? Do they need vocalization mechanisms or are they going to communicate telepathically? Do they need to walk or will they fly or teleport from place to place? Every location and, therefore, every body-form, is unique.

How is the community of souls organized? The phrase "God-Force" has been used by you to describe the universe of souls. Why do you say "God" in this instance, as there is no God?

"We have used that term in some of our writings because we answer all questions in the language, and with the degree of understanding, of the audience. In order for some people to feel the majesty of our being, only a reference to something they hold most reverent would give them an idea of the concept. Your planet has raised the majority of your youth with the belief that there exists a God who is ultimately responsible for everything that happens. He is the Judge of right and wrong and hands out rewards and punishments. Source, or God-force, is the ultimate—even though it does not judge. It is a way to get people into understanding the importance, if not the exact nature, of Source."

[See the final chapter for an essay on the existence of God.]

Is there a hierarchy running a universal organization?

"An organization implies that there is a structure, a set of rules, and a responsible element. A hierarchy involves a grading, or a judgment, that some are better than others. Since we are all one, we can't say that a part of us is better than any other. Since each part has freedom of choice, it makes its own decision concerning what it wants to experience."

Do souls use any standard to evaluate their own progress? If so, in what ways?

"We really love your language. To ask a question about our evaluation of the choices we make, you have to use a judgment term: 'standard.' This represents just how judgment- or ego-based is your society. Everything each soul does is because it wants to. If it chooses to go to Earth to learn all about control, it may start with your slavery issue. First as the slave and then as the slave master. Those two lives may satisfy the soul's curiosity. But this minimal foray into control is not a complete examination of the issue, even if it is sufficient for this soul. It would not be able to help others as a 'master of control' because it had not explored all the possibilities. If it spent many lives learning the subtleties of control from physical, mental, and emotional aspects, it would then be available to assist other souls considering the issue to set up their own experiment."

Life at Home

People have claimed knowledge of teaching areas, a library, fields of flowers, classrooms, various dimensional levels at which souls live. Is there a physical element that corresponds with any such stories, or are they manifested by individuals as personal illusions?

"Souls are all-powerful, all-creative, all-knowing; they may establish whatever scene, location, or stage that is necessary for them to do their work, or where they feel comfortable. If it is perceivable by the human psyche, it is an illusion—but then your entire physical existence is an illusion: you create the reality you desire to experience what you want.

"The most common element people see is a library, sometimes called the Akashic Library, where they may go to examine the history of what they, or others, have done in the past. It is an energetic place—that is, it is non-physical, and yet is visualized in any way that the visitor feels is comfortable. When the soul is ready, it may access the information and bring it into its current life. At Home this same knowledge is part of the awareness of the soul, who merely needs to remember what is there.

"Classrooms are a part of both the physical and non-physical worlds. In the physical world, souls may go to a classroom that allows them to analyze, or get some idea of, the meaning behind their life. This is done while day-dreaming, sleeping, or anytime the body does not need the consciousness to function. During physical sleep, souls may return to discuss with friends or advisors what they are doing. This is generally to ensure that they are following the plan they set out before they incarnated. As their awareness of essence returns, they may also visit to bring back past wisdom.

"Once returned to the energetic state, souls may need to work through the experiences they have just had, and they will always find plenty of souls with similar experiences who will help them understand the lessons behind their feelings. Some feel most comfortable if the place resembles the Earth, where they have recently resided. If a soul passes out of its body with the intention to meet another soul in a particular place, such as a field of flowers or a favorite vacation spot, it can recreate that for their reunion. Anything is possible."

You have stated that souls are wholly without gender. Is there any specific energetic activity at Home that parallels human sexual activity? Please refer also to twin flames.

"Simply stated, no. Only on Earth, in the duality, are there two types of bodies. One of the reasons for the Earth experience is to sample and play around with the reproductive experience—okay, for the neurological activity which you call the sex act!

"To have the orgasmic sexual experience, one needs to have a nervous system that responds to stimuli, accompanied by the various tactile skin receptors that trigger emotional and anatomical reactions. While those in the midst of a human life think they could not live without sex, they don't spend that much time revering it at Home. Unconditional love is much more pervasive and satisfying. It lasts forever, not just for the fraction of time sex takes. Being at Home parallels having that state of excitement, fulfillment, and love which comes at the moment of sexual release.

"The height of satisfaction at Home is joining into the energy connection with all the other souls, particularly the one known as their twin flame. The twin flame is the last particle from which a soul split off, and is as close to being identical as possible; twin flames complete each other."

Souls give reports of jobs they do at Home, e.g., welcoming returning souls, working with akashic records, acting as guides. What is the range of such activities?

"One of the desired states for souls when they return Home is to remember everything about who they are, and everything about the wisdom they gathered in all of their experiences, not only the most recent one. It is not always possible for the soul to acclimate immediately into the One, and give up its lonely individuality. Sometimes souls get on rapidly with this task, and other times they need time to rid themselves of the residual energy of their human—or other species—lives.

"Souls who have brought themselves back into balance, and who are not engaged in being debriefed about a recent experience or busy planning for an incarnation, will make themselves available to help others who are having difficulty in one of these tasks. Sometimes it is even necessary to recreate the incarnate experience and bring the person along gradually until they are ready to accept their divinity once more."

Do souls have an equivalent of sleep for their renewal?

"Renewal? What do you think a soul would have to renew? Granted, a body does need to be nourished and allowed to regenerate its precious resources. A soul is energy, and energy does not change its state of being. It continues on and on, neither increasing nor decreasing in magnitude. We are better than the Energizer Bunny—we keep going and going and going."

Are some souls bigger in energy and importance? Is the equality of souls correct in terms of essence but not true when viewed in terms of function/seniority/maturity?

"This is another Earth concept that is hard to explain in terms of souls. If a person is born in Germany and speaks German, and another in France and speaks French, another in England speaking English, is one any better or more important than the other?

"Each soul has freedom of choice to do whatever it chooses to do. One may want to spend the equivalent of lifetimes watching the way the tectonic plates move about on Earth. Another may repeatedly incarnate to learn all about abusive situations, to master all the aspects of abuse. At the end of the same number of lifetimes, or amount of Earth time, the one who went to Earth is a master of a negative lesson which they can use to help all other souls, who have not spent time thus engaged, to understand.

"All souls are composed of the same energy, the same amount of that energy, and the ability to use it as they wish. Some choose to exert themselves as much as possible, like a marathon runner, and help thousands of other souls at once. Others like to work one on one at an easy, leisurely pace.

"We all respect the choices of others. All souls are the same; some have had more experiences, which allow them to assist in more ways. You may say that we have different functions, more lives on Earth (what metaphysicians call 'an older soul') possibly equating to seniority at least in Earth matters, and you may even say that those who have worked to become masters at one or more things are more mature. But all those distinctions really mean nothing because each soul has freedom of choice and can choose to reverse roles with someone else at any time."

Concerning incarnation

The human experience appears to be attractive for souls. What is it that mostly drives them to incarnate: duty to Source, personal growth, experience of physicality?

"Since each soul is a piece of Source, it might be said that duty to Source is a reason. You should think of that duty as being to yourself as a soul, and the desires for experience that you have determined you need. It is not a duty to another person, being, or energy, since you have total control over yourself.

"Learning lessons is part of personal growth, so that would be a reason as well. Being able to exist in a duality and find out about your supreme essence while there is a challenging trip many wish to take. And, of course, being contained in a physical body that has all the nerve endings and emotional responses that are not duplicated anywhere else is a big, enticing motive to go to Earth."

Does the soul have a defined task to reach an ascending level of maturity during its repeated incarnations?

"There is nothing engraved in stone. Freedom of choice is always in operation. If a soul goes to Earth planning on learning as much about a lesson as possible, so that it would be considered a master of that lesson, the only pressure to do so is self-generated. Souls can do as much or as little as they choose in each subsequent lifetime. Resting, or diverting to another lesson from the grind of repeated stress, is also acceptable. Simply put, there are no rules."

While souls exercise freedom in making choices for their incarnation, there appears to be a well-worn track they must follow: consulting with their Council; making contractual arrangements; choosing homeland, parents, involvement in group exercises (e.g., Hitler's regime); and, on their return, debriefing and life review.

"Souls have total freedom of choice. They do not *have* to do anything. But not being unaware of what others have done, and having an idea what they think they may like to try, they consult some of those who have had similar experiences. If you are going to go to a foreign country which you know nothing about, doesn't it make sense to consult people who have lived there and know the most interesting places and things to do? And if there is a group that knows you well, and has worked with you in the past, doesn't it make sense to consult them as well? Doesn't an athlete have a coach?

"Contracts are made to ensure performance. Souls want various situations to occur, so they 'stack the deck' [with contracts] to make sure those cards are going to appear. Don't you have to purchase tickets to the places you want to go and events in which you want to participate? And location, location, location is very important, as realtors say. If you are not in the right location you will miss the opportunity. If you want to be part of a tsunami, living in the middle of a desert will not give you that chance. Being in the majority population in a country will also not let you experience discrimination against minorities. So pre-choices of homeland and parents may be vitally important.

"Going back to our statement about freedom of choice, our hypothetical incarnating soul may want to do everything itself. It may decide to have a multitude of lessons and not make any contracts to finalize their occurrence. Or it may decide to do things that need careful planning, but become overwhelmed by the onslaught of a deluge of different events. Its advisors would have suggested it might be taking on more than it could handle—but it didn't consult them. It's at a time like this that the soul throws up his hands, saying, 'I can't do all this,' and then commits suicide so it can start all over again.

"When a soul completes an incarnation, it returns home somewhat in a daze from all the sensory input it has just endured. This is when advisors, friends, and mates can help it to talk through the experience and come to appreciate what it has accomplished. How many times have you better understood something you have done after you have either talked it out with a friend, written it down in your diary, or worked through each step in your head? This is a process called 'claiming.' You acknowledge to yourself and to others that you have done something and it is now a part of your history."

What is the structure of the organization facilitating reincarnation?
"We are not sure exactly what you are asking. We have no organization. The process of incarnation is the act of going to planet Earth to see what it is like to have the choice between the positive and negative aspects of lessons and to see if, in learning these lessons, you can reconnect with your own Source energies. It is the singular choice of each separate soul. Granted, there are times when a group of souls will join together to have a major impact on the current population of the Earth, to create Earth-shattering

events. But it is the choice of each whether or not to participate. No one is told to do this or that."

It is our turn to be puzzled by your answer. We have often been told that in some way the process of incarnation has been facilitated by others who select a short list of future parents from which a soul may choose. Someone decides when a soul is not assigned to a fetus because of a probable abortion. You told us how car drivers were on a bridge to make sure they died as pre-arranged. Who does this preparation and support work?

"To facilitate is to make easier or to help something happen. This is the action of advisors and soul mates who help the soul decide exactly what it wishes to do and help it find the contacts to make contracts to have the thing happen. The counselor may have done some research to find out, in Earth terms, what type of parent will facilitate a particular experience. Having also seen what lessons the soul wants to learn and the timing desired, they see who is available for mating and then suggest possible scenarios or the choice of physical parents.

"The situation with a possible abortion is a unique occurrence. All souls have freedom of choice, and since a mother may choose to abort a fetus, which would prevent the desires of the soul to have a viable body available, that is taken into consideration from the start and uncertainty is part of the journey. When it is known that the mother has planned to have an abortion as a life lesson, it would be senseless to have a soul on hand for the fetus when it is never going to be born—so a soul never chooses to commit. The soul has complete freedom of choice—so even after decisions are initially made, they may be changed. In the case of a soul's choosing a fetus and then deciding it is not ready to go to Earth, if another soul does not wish to step in, the fetus will be stillborn.

"With the bridge and transition out of the body, the individual soul decides when it wants to return Home. Its unconscious higher self ensures that it is where it wished to be in order to participate in the death of its body. Once the incarnation takes place, all preparations for desired experiences are outlined and set into play. The only support work is in other souls' completing the contracts they agreed to perform."

Why do so many souls have difficulty deciding to come Home?

"Once a soul gets used to the sensory input from its physical nervous system, experiencing fantastic episodes of bliss, elation, and happiness, it doesn't want to leave the body and go somewhere else. Human persons who have been very involved in religious teaching may be feeling that they are about to be judged for every little thing they have done 'wrong' for their entire life, and they don't want to go there. Those who have an extremely close connection to another human who would be left behind—one they love, feel responsible for, or feel obligated to—may decide that they need to stay for that person's sake. And a final factor is the old fear of the unknown! If souls have been unable to connect to their unconditional loving essence while in human form, they don't want to take the chance of some unpleasant destination."

Aliens and Earthlings

Popular culture on Earth suggests that so-called "aliens" may be dangerous, violent, and ready to give "Earthlings" no end of trouble. Is there any truth in this, or are people on planet Earth more likely to be the bad guys?

"Of all the inhabited places in the physical realm, only planet Earth exists as a duality of positive and negative energies. Most of the other habitations are dedicated to exploring only one sort of life, e.g., communication, physical stamina or prowess, genetics, physiological responses to stimuli, transportation, and interpersonal relationships. There is a group that is studying war strategies, but that is only one out of thousands. The majority of all these beings belong to a consortium that believes each planet's inhabitants need to find their own way without interference from others who have grown beyond them. You may remember this theme from the 'Prime Directive' in Gene Roddenberry's *Star Trek* series. Gene had a lot of advisors on this side whom he constantly ran ideas by, and had help remembering the way things are.

"The whole idea about aliens being evil stems from your entertainment industry and the fear of the unknown. Because humans live with dramas like *V*, where they are being set up to be conquered and used by the aliens, a large portion of the industrialized world see interlopers as bad. The military thought process involves always being ready to triumph, so some say, 'Shoot first and ask questions later.' You do have an aggressive stance against the unknown abilities of new encounters. The arrogance of humans—that someone is always trying to better them—makes you trigger happy. There are too many variables to make a definitive statement about who will strike first; but, yes, Earthlings are more likely to be the bad guys."

How often do people from outside visit the planet in a physical form?
"Probably more often than anyone would guess. Earth is a terrific tourist attraction. Imagine being able to visit a planet that does things to cause its own self-destruction. It is fun to watch the blame game take place and, at the same time, see whole nations mobilize to help another in distress. It is better than visiting an amusement park dedicated to life. situations.

"A number of the species have the ability to shift their vibration slightly so they become invisible to humans. This allows them to stand right in the midst of any decision-making process without being observed. Others do not need to land on Earth, but stay in orbit and watch just like the military satellites. You, too, are watchers through your televisions. You have a front row seat for all major events and disasters. Think how interested you are in what is going on and you will get a feeling of how outsiders are just as intrigued."

How significant is the monitoring of life on Earth from the Other Side?

"Are you implying that souls at Home are aliens? Souls have just as much curiosity about happenings on Earth, and other places, as someone enjoying a physical existence. We don't interfere for the same reasons most aliens choose not to interact. Personal guides may seek to get the attention of their friend, but they can't interfere without an invitation."

What do souls gain from their monitoring and visiting the planet?

"The first thing that is gained is information—knowledge—and then, perhaps, wisdom. To observe another is to do research into possibilities. They are checking on something they might want to do later themselves. They may learn if someone has found a way to accomplish a lesson they were unable to complete, or observe just to be entertained. When beings have not previously chosen to spend a life in the duality of Earth, they may wish to see what the intensity level would feel like for them."

Do they come in spaceships as have been commonly reported?

"Yes, the majority do travel in some sort of craft. Others have the ability to teletransport from their living place to Earth without the need of a vehicle or the expenditure of time. Some beings can also open a hole between their place and yours and stroll through. Others remain at their home planet and watch a projection as if they were present.

"When it comes to space ships, those of you who believe in their existence have been watching their antics for years. In order to see something, you have to first acknowledge to yourself that it can and does exist. If you deny the existence of aliens, you will never be able to see them because your brain will not process what your eyes are seeing. If you live your life open to all possibilities, you will be able to see all that is around you—including alien visitors."

How are spaceships constructed and powered?

"The physical craft come in all sorts of configurations. The initial factor in their manufacture is the atmosphere encountered from the home planet to Earth. Does the ship need to be an atmospheric bubble to sustain their life-form? Next is the duration of any trip from point of origin to destination: will it take a short hop, or what we know as years to traverse the universe? If we are talking a long haul, then the spaceship must have a means of producing life-sustaining materials such as food, moisture, and air if they are necessary to maintain survival of the species.

"Many materials are used, of which you have no knowledge because they do not exist on your planet. Power sources are numerous. Some are derivatives of nuclear propulsion, but, again, most of you could not possibly conceive of them for they are a long way beyond your experience. It is possible for a number of conveyances to be powered by the intention of the mind. No fossil fuels here, folks!"

The soul and the higher mind

You have said that the soul incarnates by pouring itself into every cell in the body. What then is the relationship of the soul and the unconscious, or so-called "higher mind"?

"The mind, as you seem to be referring to it here, is synonymous with the contents of the brain matter. The brain is merely a hard-drive storage facility that records all the data to which the human body's eyes and ears have been exposed. When the brain is consulted it can only regurgitate, and sometimes extrapolate, from what is stored within. The higher mind, higher self, or subconscious, is a non-physical aspect of the soul wherein prior experience knowledge is stored and accessed. This is not readily available to the brain or conscious mind.

"The soul, in joining with the body, prepares itself to start a new life, similar to a new career, while maintaining the ability to consult and retreat into a prior life or use wisdom stored from the past careers. Since the knowledge would only confuse and delay the new endeavor if it had to be waded through to find the next step in learning a current lesson, it is held in abeyance out of the conscious stream of thought. Every cell is engaged in the learning process and, when stimulated, can trigger the conscious mind to go looking for an experience in the unconscious that will aid in its task. This is accomplished by going into the feelings a person possesses of what—hidden inside—is needed to solve the problem.

"When people seem stuck in their progress through life, or feel unbalanced, they can retrieve answers from the unconscious. This is easily done with the assistance of a hypnotherapist, but may also be done by the people themselves. By entering into a deep meditation, where the conscious mind is disengaged, the soul may be consulted to problem-solve. If people have difficulty shutting down their thinking mind, just before they retire, they may put a question to their unconscious mind, which takes over in sleep."

It seems odd that we seek to know our soul with the part of us, the ego, that dies with the body. When a human being seeks to know its soul better, is this essentially a matter of educating the ego, or is it rather to explore the attitude of the ego in order to educate the soul?

"We have constantly mentioned that the ego is the 'god' of the third dimension—that aspect of the physical experience where everything is judged and graded. When we talked about your purpose as getting to know your true essence, we just assumed you would have realized it could not to be done using a grading process. What you should seek to understand your divine, non-physical nature with, is the sense organs which are only contained in the body you inhabit while incarnate. And the place you go to do this is in the heart-based, *feeling* soul as it emerges from the control of the third-dimensional, *thinking* ego. You must put aside judgment and start using non-ego evaluation for your observation of this possible, fantastic part of life.

"In the essence form we share with you, we know only unconditional love and bliss. We cannot evaluate just how magnificent and precious that is until we know what it is not. If you have only lived in Iceland, you do not know what it is like to live in Tahiti. You know only cold, a predominance of darkness, and swirling winds. Taking a trip to Tahiti will introduce you to balmy warm breezes, lots of sunshine, going with little clothing so you can feel the warmth of the sun, and feeling the beauty of sharing the sea with colorful marine animals. You may then evaluate where you wish to spend more time without entering into a judgment that one is better than the other—they are just different places that allow you to have divergent learning experiences.

"The purpose of the soul, after learning the lessons it incarnated to accomplish, is to know as much as it can about its own essence, to be able to experience the feeling of unconditional love in the arena of a living, breathing human body with all its sensory instruments. At this point in the soul's life cycle, when it is working on its ultimate purpose, it has given up the need to judge ego aspects of life. Unconditional love cannot be perceived by the ego, because it is love impossible to judge. Therefore, you do not seek to know your soul using your ego. While still ego-driven, the thought of a possible non-physical soul does not even arise within the ego's field of inquiry.

"Everything the soul encounters in an incarnation, whether ego- or heart-driven, adds to its plethora of knowledge. The ego ceases to exist with the termination of the body, but the information gleaned does not cease to be remembered."

Thank you, Masters.

~ * ~

Making Changes

According to the Ascended Masters' metaphysical teaching, to understand reincarnation correctly we must be prepared to make major changes in our thinking. We must now look at human life in a way that is significantly different from the view of traditional religions, ethical systems, and quantum physics. Even New Age spiritualism is seen as containing a substantial amount of speculation.

God and Source

The principal issue that we must consider in the Masters' sayings concerns the existence of God, as described and believed in many religions. One of our enquirers wrote to us with a simple question: *"Masters, I sometimes doubt the existence of God. How can I believe what I do not see?"* Their answer was as follows:

"It is common within the human race to need validation for the beliefs and standards it has set for itself. The human world is controlled by the ego, which constantly needs to judge one thing against another to determine an individual's 'worth.' To judge, you have to see and be able to grade. If you cannot select an item and compare its qualities with any other item, it is worthless. The invisible or non-physical must be ignored since it is not gradable. That is the mantra of society.

"People never include in their grading system emotional things affecting their lives. Love cannot be seen or

227

compared, yet it is acknowledged to exist. Many people live their lives based upon love. Powerful, body-impacting emotions are also not within the visual spectrum, yet they result in tears, laughter, headaches, stomach pains—all felt in the physical body. Smells are another confusing phenomenon: it is possible to distinguish thousands of different scents but you cannot see, hold, or photograph them. We would ask you: do any of these things therefore exist?

"There are also energetic materials on your planet that have a major impact on your lives. Not only can you not see these materials, you cannot even fully explain how they exist. The most common of these is electricity. It is invisible; it has no odor, no color, and no feel of its own—unless you happen to get in the way of its travelling from one place to another. You use it every day. Your life would not be pleasant without its availability. But prove to us it exists without also showing us what it can do; try to find a definition of what electricity is, and you will discover that even your experts cannot define it.

"Everything we have discussed so far is accepted by people as having always been around during their lifetime. One thing all of these elements have in common is a *source*. Emotions are a response to thought processes occurring in your heads. They produce a visceral reaction in your physical body. Smells usually can be traced back to a physical object that gives off a signature invisible vapor. An electric current can be produced by exciting electrons. Each one of them has a source.

"The universe and everything within it has a Source. Organized religions call this point of origin by the names God, Mohammad, Allah, Yahweh, Brahma, Vishnu, just to mention a few. If you researched what the world considers God to be, one answer might read that God is a name in English given to an exceptional being in theistic and deistic religions, and other faiths, who is either the exclusive deity in monotheism or a single deity in polytheism. Does that help? We rather doubt it.

"The whole problem with using the expression 'God' is that the historic beliefs that tag along have to be accepted to give you an idea of what you are supposed to believe. Generally, God is first presented to you as the power behind the existence of man. Almost always portrayed as masculine, God is usually seen with long, grayish-white hair and beard, and attired in a white robe. God is seen as the one who hands out rewards and punishments for following the rules that He has given to man. He is the ultimate judge of the disposition of your soul after your mortal existence. His ordained ministers are His representatives on this Earth and must be obeyed as He is to be followed—without question.

"If you have followed all the rules and been a good person, you may pray, appeal, beseech Him to allow a change to occur in the course of ongoing actions that you want to escape. None of the beliefs in a God-based system talks of individuals having freedom of choice to determine their own eternal future. Is this the God in whose existence you have trouble believing?

"We know that people on your planet are particles of a Source material that existed before all else. The essence of 'Source' is a sentient, all-encompassing substance that is the origin of the energy out of which everything in the universe is made. It wanted to know more about itself, so pieces were broken off that could go and experience what it, as the universal Source, could not. Each one of these fragments, which were called souls, had all the same qualities and abilities of which Source is composed.

"Then Earth came into being. Earth is a place of duality where there exists an interactive polar opposite for all things. Within a human lifetime on Earth, each soul has the opportunity to choose which sides of each action it wants to experience. The soul has the power to make these decisions as long as it has accepted responsibility for its life and not ceded that power to another—such as a group who tells it how to think and behave.

"When it comes down to the existence or non-existence of things that comprise your reality, *you* are the determining agent. Do you base your beliefs on the belief of others? Or do you reach inside and feel what resonates with your being? If you only ask yourself what you think—rather than feel—about something, you are merely going into your head and reviewing what has already been planted there. Almost everything in your memory came in through your ears and eyes from other people. If, instead, you go into your heart to discover your feelings, you are effectively asking yourself: 'Does this feel like something I can accept without taking a poll of my friends, family, and society?'

"When you were a child, you were taken care of by adults and told what was right and wrong, as they interpreted it. As you grew, you began to see that some things that made you fearful as a child were only so because you were not experienced enough to make adequate decisions for your own protection. It was difficult at first to start assuming responsibility for all the daily decisions you had to make in life. When as a child you had others to make the decisions for you, you could never be wrong—it was always someone else's fault!

"Start making your own reality. Take everything in your life, including the basic principles of existence that you don't normally think about, such as the existence of a God, and see how you feel about each. Keep those that feel that they are a part of the fabric of your being. Discard those that don't fit. When making decisions, take your power back from all those to whom you have given that ability in the past. Don't let others tell you what to think—and definitely not what to believe.

"Remember: You are a piece of Source and have the ability to tap into the wisdom garnered throughout the ages—you only have to decide to open the door."

(The Masters)

Does this make us atheists?

It cannot ever be said that the Masters suggest we become atheists, even though "God" is a word they only seem to use in a religious context when it is necessary to get a point across to someone. God, in the view of religion, is a person. This is, they assert, where the error begins. We have taken an ancient anthropomorphic myth that portrays the Creator to be a man-god person. But there is no real substance in this belief. The god or gods of the world's religions do not provide any hard, verifiable evidence for their creation and their sustaining of the universe. It is entirely preferable to accept that Source is an energetic force, and that its essence may even resemble the vision of physicists who say that energetic sub-atomic particles, in strings or waves, are that creative First Cause of the universe.

Nevertheless, although quantum physics may be closer to a correct answer, it will never reach its goal without our help. While it is true that physical science has discovered an element of reactive sentience within sub-atomic particles in the lab, it takes a step into quantum metaphysics to understand it fully. The prime cause—the physicists' "Answer for Everything"—we in metaphysics imbue with a quality that few respectable scientists would ever attempt to verify. We see the primary life-giving particles of Source energy as having two distinct aspects. The first is that it is everywhere, in everything—that's the physics of it. But Source is also the highest, most perfect element in the realm not only of physical matter, but also of thought and feeling, both of which are energetic but cannot be verified by the scientific method. Source energy is without limitation and unconditional because it is the ultimate in positive energy.

What shall we call the energy in thought and feeling? Unscientifically yet, we believe, meaningfully we call it "love." Before rejecting the word love, scientists need to find a better word that fits the concept of the most positive element—both for matter and for purely energetic thoughts and feelings. Of course we can choose to call that element "X" rather than "Love." Yet in a sense human language has already committed us to the answer. Love is designated in our speech as the most positive, most deeply creative, most truly thoughtful feeling human beings possess. A thought or feeling that is less than "unconditionally loving" does not fit our conncept of the ultimate. So far as we are concerned people can call this element-in-everything "X." After all words are only words. "That which we call a rose by any other name would smell as sweet." But the reality is that in thought and feeling society *has* named it otherwise. So, let scientific scruples be overcome: "love is all you need."

We are not atheists. We tell the world that Source was, and is, and will be ever the same. It is the creative energy in every atom of the universe and the ultimate positive element that enables thought and feeling. Source love radiates in our soul because each one of us is a fragment of Source. We cannot live as human beings without soul, which is the embodiment of Source. What we do deny is that Source is a *person*. It is energy; it is eternal. It is our essence.

Doing without judgment

A major change in our thinking must follow. Unconditional love is non-judgmental. In the spiritual Home there is no right or wrong, no good or bad, no correct or incorrect.

The concept of God as the final arbiter of rewards for lives well lived, and of punishment for those badly lived, is discarded as plain wrong, along with the out-of-date portrait of God as a person. In the spirit realm beyond our planet there is no heaven, the place of reward; no purgatory, the place of cleansing; no hell, the place of punishment. These are concepts alive and well on planet Earth but nowhere else.

Singled out for special treatment, planet Earth, the duality of positivity versus negativity held equally in energetic balance, is where heaven and hell truly exist. Hell is found in the negative things people do to each other that can drive not only victims but also perpetrators into torment within their minds. Heaven, as well, is a state of blissful being for us only while we are on the planet or within the interface between Earth and Home.

God is never seen by our guides as the great Judge of humankind. While souls can and do imagine themselves judged for what they may have done, it is the ego-driven basis of human thinking that puts such things into neat categories. Our conscious minds are limited in terms of their creativity as a side effect of duality, and so have developed neat, ethical ways of separating the good from the bad, sheep from goats, and saints from sinners.

Having a purpose

In their answers to our questions, the Masters have painted a picture of the reason why our souls have incarnated. Shakespeare spoke of all the world being a stage and "all the men and women merely players." This is a very close parallel to the life of the soul on planet Earth. We come of our own free will, with our personal circumstances and the role we have chosen to play outlined in advance. We ask for and are given various trials that we call life lessons. The

Masters often call human life "an illusion." It is illusory for a soul, whose essence is unconditional love, to play the part of a Hitler, a serial murderer, or even, less socially harmful, a schizophrenic or cancer patient.

When we incarnate, we play various roles *in order to experience negativity*, and out of that experience to gain a deeper understanding of what we ourselves are not and never will be. This role play absolves our soul from the charge of doing evil—that belongs to the human role we play. There can be no judgment levied on us as a soul, apart from our self-assessment of whether we played the chosen role to the best of our ability. There will be no judgment made by our peers; other souls are interested in the way we are handling our life as a soul, but we are all by inner nature perfectly loving—and "love keeps no score of wrongs."

Our purpose is to discover ourselves more fully in the contrast provided by all kinds of negativity. It is the desire of Source to know its magnificence more truly, and we, as fragments of Source, are at one with its quest for wisdom.

Being an eternal soul

The most religious-sounding aspect of our being is that we are pure energy and, for that reason, never change or decay. Traditional faith declares our souls to be eternal, although most of the time it is the heavenly reward or hellish punishment that is declared to be everlasting! But the Masters remind us that our eternal aspect, matched by our creativity, is a factor in the here and now, and not only after we have transitioned Home.

Where we notice the importance on Earth of our eternal aspect is mainly in relation to our birth and death. The provision of the energetic soul incarnate in the fetus ensures that it will live. No one lives, outside of the maternal womb, without having the energy of life provided by a soul.

This is equally applicable to questions of abortion, suicide, life-support, and euthanasia, that we have examined in this book. It is the vital state of the soul that avoids the death of the body when it dies, and permits the soul to cross over from the third dimension of human life on Earth to the spiritual Home as and when it desires.

There is another, less well recognized, element in the fact of the soul's being eternal and unconditionally loving. It possesses wisdom far in excess of the wisdom of the human ego. The human mind is a computer, driven by data entry and search for answers. The higher mind of the soul has an understanding and an ability to assess the truth of situations that is far superior. The ideal life of the human is to be lived with as much awareness of the soul's direction and comfort as possible. If we fail to live by the prompting of our instincts, we are not living to the full.

Conclusion

We are glad you have come this far with us in our exploration of reincarnation. We have considered ourselves most fortunate to have been invited by the Masters to be their voice and to advance their teaching in the written word. We hope that this book has given you an overview of the issues, and that you "feel"—the word they would have us always use—that there is some merit in our account of their core teaching.

We have more books for you to consider, mostly of a different kind, involving us in channeled interviews with both well known and unknown souls. We hope you will be able to enjoy using them in following up your exploration of the concept of reincarnation. Remember to feel the answers that are within you and avoid people who want to do the thinking for you. There are people using spirituality for personal advantage—and don't let anyone (including us) dictate how you should think.

Please share this precious knowledge with others. The Masters do not intend to set up a member organization. It's up to anyone who wishes to support their work to introduce their teaching to family and friends.

We wish you love, light, and laughter.

~ * ~

Studying Reincarnation

Toni Ann Winninger and Peter Watson Jenkins have created the Spirit Masters' blog and a Facebook page dedicated to the study of their teaching, and to giving spiritual assistance in their answers to questions from a worldwide audience. Remember "Reincarnation Guide" and you will find it easy to access their blog at www.ReincarnationGuide.com, and daily entries on Facebook: Reincarnation Guide.

Books and ebooks, offered by the Masters' publishers at www.CelestialVoicesInc.com, include the following:

How I Died (and what I did next)
>Accounts by 28 souls of their various experiences of transition from Earth to Home. (Book and ebook)

Spirit World Wisdom
>Selections from messages received from the Spirit Masters in a three-and-a-half-year period. (Book and ebook)

Healing with the Universe, Meditation, and Prayer
>An ebook featuring a discussion of self-healing, different healing methods, and an analysis of prayers from world religions.

Dialogues with Masters of the Spirit World—a trilogy

I. Talking with Leaders of the Past (Book and ebook)
>The Masters' discussion of reincarnation is followed by dialogues with the souls of 15 prominent people born in the nineteenth

century: Andrew Carnegie, Winston S. Churchill, Charles Darwin, Albert Einstein, Mahatma Gandhi, Adolf Hitler, William James, Pope John XXIII, Carl Jung, Dwight Moody, Florence Nightingale, Eleanor Roosevelt, Bertrand Russell, Margaret Sanger, and Oscar Wilde.

II. *Talking with Twentieth-Century Women* (Book and ebook)

Dialogues with the souls of 21 prominent women: Jane Addams, Marian Anderson, Maria Callas, Rachel Carson, Marie Curie, Amelia Earhart, Ella Fitzgerald, Anne Frank, Judy Garland, Barbara Jordan, Helen Keller, Margaret Mead, Golda Meir, Carmen Miranda, Marilyn Monroe, Georgia O'Keeffe, Selena Quintanilla-Perez, Sylvia Plath, Wilma Rudolph, Sharon Tate, and Mother Teresa.

III. *Talking with Twentieth-Century Men* (Book and ebook)

Dialogues with the souls of 21 prominent men: Frank Lloyd Wright, Pablo Picasso, George S. Patton, Babe Ruth, Ernest Hemingway, Walt Disney, Louis Armstrong, George Orwell, Robert Oppenheimer, Jesse Owens, Joe Louis, Frank Sinatra, Yehudi Menuhin, Sam Walton, James Baldwin, Peter Sellers, Cesar E. Chavez, Andy Warhol, Martin Luther King, Jr., Elvis Presley, John Lennon.

Our bookstore:

www.CelestialVoicesInc.com

All paperback and ebook editions

Titles are also available in paperback at Amazon and bookstores in Australia, Britain, Canada, and the United States. Ebooks are available for electronic readers at: Apple, Diesel, Kindle, Kobo, Nook, Sony, and Smashwords.

CPSIA information can be obtained at www.ICGtesting.com
Printed in the USA
237639LV00004B/19/P